GROWING UP
IN OZ

❖ ❖ ❖

George M. Radcliffe, Jr.

ISBN 978-1-62806-369-1 (print | hardcover)

Library of Congress Control Number 2023901326

Published by Salt Water Media
29 Broad Street, Suite 104
Berlin, Maryland 21811
www.saltwatermedia.com

Salt-Water
MEDIA

Cover design by Brian Robertson

GROWING UP
IN OZ

CONTENTS

PROLOGUE:

THE PICTURE ON OUR STAIRCASE

Every day I pass a photo of my childhood family as I ascend my staircase. Ours was an unusual but loving family of which I am the lone surviving member. Standing behind my father in that photo, I was the oldest child. That eight-year-old had no idea what lay in store for him and certainly did not expect to be the lone survivor of the four children when he was just thirty-two. My parents had to see three of their four children die in their lifetime, and I watched them suffer their remaining years, praying that they would not outlive all their children; I, however, feel far more joy than regret. When a loved one dies, there is a tendency for the living to focus on what they have lost. I treasure what I have. What is sad, however, is that my siblings could be forgotten over time. None had children who would pass on memories, stories, or their DNA. Gone over forty years now, they are remembered by few, but they are alive and well inside of me. Not a day goes without some memory of them lighting a smile on my face. My life has become a memorial to them, and this book is my attempt to help keep them alive for others. I dedicate this book to that family of six, an unusual and sometimes dysfunctional family, but then that describes all real families. While we were all flawed, that is what made us so delightfully human. However, we were still a strong family bonded by love.

Gussie (1951 – 1982) and Bill (1953 – 1982) both died in the same car accident, and my sister Kim (1957 – 1975) died far too young from pneumonia. Gussie, born with a significant congenital circulatory issue, suffered her entire short life but still brought so much joy and laughter to those around her. She lived each day with an energy that wore out the rest of us. Bill was an award-winning newspaper journalist whose career was cut down before it could take off. With an incredible imagination and sense of humor, he could amuse himself in any situation. My parents quickly learned that confining him to his room was not a punishment as he would soon be engaged in some activity while he laughed and sang. Kim was born mentally handicapped (then called mental retardation), but she was pure joy and a pivotal part of my early life.

I also dedicate this to my beloved wife Jackie, who has put up with a less-than-perfect human for fifty-two years. Meeting and marrying her was the defining piece of my life. I've often wondered what would have happened if I had not taken that blind date in February 1969. She has become my guiding light and strength, and my life has been blessed with her.

The Radcliffe Family
November 1957

A Letter to My Grandchildren: Growing Up In Oz

To my beloved grandchildren ... Like most children, you probably view your grandfather as a confident adult, but like all of us, I did not begin that way. I started as a diaper-wearing, nose-running, crying infant, and some might say that was the high point of my life. I could never picture my parents or grandparents as children; I only knew the finished product, refined by a lifetime of trial and error. You also don't realize that your grandfather grew up in Oz. Like Dorothy's Oz, it was a delightful land full of beautiful adventures and colorful individuals, but it had its dark side—demons that terrified me. During the 1950s and early 1960s, I walked down my yellow brick road accompanied by a beagle, a teddy bear, and a remarkable family. It was a magical, if not real, journey presided over by four wizards and haunted by several demons. In Oz, I often stumbled but was allowed the freedom to grow as an individual. I would find out later that Oz was not the real world, but I treasure the memories from those wonderful days.

My Oz was initially a tiny community of three-story row houses bordering an extremely narrow one-way, nicely shaded road. Situated in a dark valley between two tall apartment mountain peaks, near Johns Hopkins University and Memorial Stadium in Baltimore, Maryland, my little world was hardly noteworthy in a city known for its many neighborhoods of row houses. Our family moved when I was nine to a larger house in the city, and although the houses were more widely spaced, the neighborhood was still a closely-knit community, populated by as many dogs as people.

Armed with screw-on roller skates, a red wagon, and a box of baseball cards, I was free to explore and deal with the world, defined by my mother as any place within two blocks of our house. I had a bicycle, which wasn't needed because of my restricted range, but it gave me the impression of freedom. Baltimore in the 1950s was America in miniature, albeit an America that was about to undergo massive change. In the 1950s, mine was a white-dominated world, primarily free of crime and insulated from what one would see on the evening news, which few children saw. It was a glorious time to grow up for those in my world. Sandwiched between World War II and the turmoil of the 1960s, a child could exist without a care. The country may have been on the verge of exploding racially, and the Cold War was looming in the background, but we were protected from seeing the world as it was, especially since few of us could afford television sets. In the aftermath of the war to end all wars, most Americans, at least those who were white, wanted to relish the freedom and prosperity they had risked their lives for. The advent of television reinforced the fantasy world many wanted to believe in, the unrealistic and simplified world of *Father Knows Best*, *Ozzie and Harriet*, and *Leave it to Beaver*. Our Oz turned out to be vastly different from reality, and we later realized that many were deprived of the opportunity to experience the real world. However, it allowed many of us to grow up in peace and freedom from the worries of the world, and while I have left Oz far behind, it remains an integral part of who I am.

Adults often paint childhood as a carefree existence, but it is challenging work: overcoming a steady stream of obstacles, learning how to fit into a fast-paced world that is hurtling by, and finding our stride. One can take courses on becoming a doctor, electrician, or teacher, but there is no manual for becoming a grown-up. It is trial and error, and while the trials can be exciting, the errors make one feel like a misfit. However, it is our errors that hasten our journey to adulthood, but dealing with errors requires perseverance and a sense of humor. In other words, I began just like you, not the refined and confident adult you know—although I'm still quite proficient at making errors. My errors in life could fill a book—in fact, several of them, and this book is just the first. The only way to ensure you never make an error is to do nothing—but then you miss out on all the joy life offers.

My life has been insignificant in some ways; I will never be in *Who's Who*, and my life will not be made into a blockbuster film. Unlike so many today, I don't seek my fifteen minutes of fame, something that is artificial and fleeting, but each of us can have influence—make the world a better place. In history books, you read about the kings, queens, presidents, generals, and inventors, but it is often the masses of people behind the scenes that make changes happen. My life has been remarkable because my Oz was based around a unique family: a strong father, a completely unselfish and loving mother, three special siblings, and four special grandparents. We were far from a perfect family, but the flaws made us real.

As in your generation, we had our heroes, our larger-than-life characters that we all idolized and aspired to be like. In the baseball world, Willie Mays, Mickey Mantle, and Brooks Robinson were heroes to many of us, but equally important were the Mercury astronauts and political leaders. Children today have their Star Wars heroes; we had the Lone Ranger, Hopalong Cassidy, and Superman. The early age of rockets and satellites made dreamers of all of us; the drama of early space travel was both exciting and terrifying as the dangers were extremely obvious to all. Most important, sports and the entertainment world gave us our first connection with races we had limited daily contact with: Jackie Robinson, Roberto Clemente, Harry Belafonte, Little Richard, Ella Fitzgerald, Sam Cooke, and Nat

King Cole. However, my real heroes were my family: my mother, who was the paramount of unselfish love, my father from whom I learned patience and a sense of humor, my sister, whom I saw attack life with passion despite monstrous physical and psychological limitations, and grandparents who taught me the importance of listening.

In Oz, we learned many valuable life lessons. There were far fewer organized activities than today, and we used our imagination and initiative to schedule a full day of adventures. We had no problem inventing games and creating experiences. We learned to be resourceful, using limited materials to construct go-carts and forts, and we could turn a simple bicycle into any conceivable form of transportation. We learned how to compromise with others as every neighborhood activity involved a degree of give and take. We visited foreign lands without ever leaving our neighborhood and traveled to other planets in spaceships we assembled out of lumber scraps we found. We put on plays regularly, acting out fantasies. It was a glorious time to be a child, and we cherished the freedom our parents granted us.

However, the most valuable lesson I learned may have come from my father's ability to find humor in any circumstance, even those wrapped in tragedy. The hardest life lesson for me may have been to learn to find humor in myself. I never suffered from an excessive ego, which paved the way for not taking myself too seriously. Ego can impede self-growth in so many cases, and self-doubt can equally retard progress. Finding and keeping the proper balance was a continuous quest.

Later in life, I was to learn the lesson that, to this day, guides me through all the obstacles that life throws at us. The oldest of four children, I would become the only survivor at an early age, and my life would be changed forever. Surprisingly, out of that tragedy came a golden nugget I never expected—every day life offers us is a gift, never to be wasted. Every morning as I stumble out of bed, I think of my siblings. Sandwiched with the sadness that they can't experience that day is the joy that I can. I live each day for the four of us, and wasting a day disrespects their memory. They are a part of me, now and forever.

To you, my grandchildren, I give you these thoughts and memories of my ordinary life. These essays cover the first few years of my life, the ones you are struggling through now. Take them for what they are, not a map to the future, but a foundation on which you build your "cathedral." No matter how dark the night or deep the hole may seem, there always is another day. Treasure each day because you can only live it once. Your future is totally in your hands, and none of us can imagine what it will bring. We lack the tools to see where progress will lead us, but we have the means to begin the search. We must, however, remain grounded in the principles which have guided us so far: a family-first mentality, the courage to confront any demons, and the ability and courage to put our best foot forward each day.

Resurrection: First Grade Style

Before anyone could stop Jack, the earth opened up,
and he dropped into the fires of hell.

Religion and I have had a rocky relationship, to say the least. My mother was a devout Catholic, and while I always respected and appreciated her religion's value, the wheels started falling off my religion cart at an early age. I'm a skeptic, an excellent tool for science but not always appreciated in the religious community. My mother's faith provided the lifelong context for dealing with many personal tragedies.

Religion started to unravel for me in the first grade when I attended a small Catholic school near our home. I was a shy and, thus, seemingly well-behaved kid, but I hadn't gotten into the private school my parents wanted for me. They gave me an entrance test and decided I was not the brightest bulb on the tree. That certainly was true, but the report listed me as having below-average intelligence. Since the test was primarily verbal, and I was shy and stuttered, one could question whether I was fairly tested.

For the next three years, I attended a school taught by cloistered nuns who had not seen the light of day since World War II since they could not go out past the walls of their convent. They were wonderful caring people, although not the most enlightened educators, and I'm not sure how well they understood young children. They said we were created in the image of God, but if they only had known what we were really like, they might have questioned the goodness of our creator. The mother superior wielded a mean yardstick which, fortunately, I had only heard about. My good friend Jack got to know it intimately. He was a good kid, but if Hank Ketchum had needed inspiration for Dennis the Menace, he needed to look no further than Jack. How someone with such good intentions could get in so much trouble baffled me even at that early age, but Jack had a heart of gold, even if his exterior was constructed of Silly Putty.

The fact that the nuns were cloistered posed numerous problems. They had to leave all their classes unsupervised briefly at Noon each day while they retreated to the convent for prayers. Leaving thirty kids unattended for ten minutes might not have been the brightest move; I don't ever remember us setting anything on fire, but we did have a sentry to warn us when Sister was hustling back down the hallway. Did she believe all that time that we just sat there silently doing our work? However, the poor nuns were in deep trouble when it came to playground supervision. They couldn't go out to our playground because it was beyond the boundaries of the monasterial world. If parent volunteers weren't available, they resorted to God's wrath, which certainly impressed six-year-olds who had memorized their catechisms and heard numerous biblical accounts of hell, fire, and damnation. I remember their often-repeated admonition ... "If you go past that hedge boundary, the earth will open up, and you will drop into the fires of hell." That got the attention of a six-year-old, and I certainly had enough intelligence and imagination to be able to visualize hell. I tried hard to conjure up an image of what lay on the other side of that hedge: an unimaginable conflagration with Satan himself presiding. If the earth opened, would we hear the screams of the many who burned away for eternity? Would we smell the burning flesh? These nuns had boned up on their Dante, which was the ultimate fodder for children's nightmares. But it worked—at least for a while.

I had burnt my hand once, and the pain had been unbearable. But to burn for eternity seemed incomprehensible. I remember lying in bed on several occasions, trying to imagine this horror. God was supposed to be a loving deity, but he apparently had no qualms about tossing away his defective "creations." Six-year-old children take things literally, and there was no doubt in my mind that the earth would have opened up if that hedge line were crossed. We all stayed far away from that hedge in the event that the teacher had been off a few feet in her estimate of where the no-man's land began.

We usually played ball close to the building; better to risk a broken window than eternal damnation, and living in the city, we had all broken our share of windows by this point in our lives. What was one more? Jack and I were playing ball that fateful day, each thinking we were the second coming of Willie Mays, while we weren't even a close approximation of a six-year-old athlete. For us, playing ball consisted of throwing it in the other person's direction and then watching them chase down the errant throw. For some reason that day, we were not playing right beside the building. Jack had a crush on Susan, one of our classmates, and we had to play near her as if she would be impressed by two little kids who couldn't even throw the ball in the right direction. After chasing down one of my throws, Jack stood closer to the hedge. After getting the ball back to me, he said, "Can you throw it this far?" It was my turn to show off, and I uncorked my best throw ever. It took off like a rocket, sailed over his head, and then ... over THE hedge. Terror quickly took over. Jack stared in disbelief at the hedge while I knew this was another ball lost forever. Then came the "conference on the mound."

As I joined Jack near the hedge, he quickly said, "I can get it," a comment meant for Susan's ears.

"Are you crazy?" I quickly chimed in. Now Jack was anything but shy, but this tempted God's wrath. "But you have heard what the nuns said." At this point, a crowd had gathered on "the mound," and the others joined my attempts to prevent the imminent incineration of Jack.

"Jack, don't do it."

"It's not worth the risk. We can get another ball."

"My brother Ted said he saw the flames once."

However, I knew the die was cast when Susan reached the group. "Please, Jack, don't do it," repeating the phrase over and over.

Jack loved being the center of attention, especially with Susan fawning over him. He was tempted to go to impress Susan, but he couldn't build up the nerve. Impressing a girl was one thing, but risking becoming a wiener in the cosmic barbecue seemed a bit much to all of us. That was until Martin, the class bully, showed up. "Jack, you don't have the guts." He also was working to win Susan's attention and admiration. "You're too chicken to go get it."

That did it. Jack knew there was only one way he could win Susan's respect. He suddenly turned and took off after the ball. Collectively we screamed, "Jack, stop…please…don't!" He kept running toward the hedge, and soon thirty six-year-old children were screaming and dissolved in tears—even Martin, who never thought Jack would give in. Susan was wailing, and the rest of us called out every admonition we could conjure up. He continued to run, reaching the hedge, and in an instant, he was gone. The group became very silent as our little imaginations filled in the gory details. Jack was toast by now.

Time elapsed, and no one knew what to do. One of the kids suggested running back to the building to get a fire extinguisher, but we all decided this might not do the job. None of us had seen the fires of hell, but it would take a little more than a pound of foam to put out that fire. No adult was present, and the group had moved from tears to hysteria. One of the little girls had run back to the building to share the tragic news with the teacher, but we figured this would elicit a quick "I told you so." I had lost a close friend, and I was distraught. If only I could have stopped him or wrestled him to the ground, but

Jack was much stronger than me. Even Susan was much stronger than me.

Suddenly the hedge parted, and Jack appeared carrying the ball. Thirty little boys and girls stared in complete disbelief. How could this be? And he didn't even seem to be burnt. A roar erupted everywhere, and all rushed up to the new class hero. You've never seen such a celebration as we all mobbed Jack; no World Series has ever ended with such jubilation. We'd have picked him up and marched him around if any of us had been strong enough. Jack loved all the celebrating, especially when he glanced over to see the adoring Susan. Jack had been to hell and back, although we were secretly disappointed to hear that the Earth had not opened and there was no fire.

For the next several days, all anyone could talk about was our class hero. We could have gotten him elected U.S. president if he had been old enough. I was thrilled to have both my friend and the ball back. Susan had her seat moved next to Jack, who was now the happiest kid on planet Earth. After several days in which all anyone could talk about was Jack's miraculous resurrection, the conversation soon shifted to why the earth hadn't swallowed Jack. The class braggart Martin finally vocalized what most of us had thought, "The nuns tricked us," followed by something that had never occurred to any of us, "There probably isn't a real hell." Our teacher quickly rebuked that comment, but the cat was now out of the bag. Martin quickly provided evidence for his radical theory by crossing the hedge line during our next recess. The Visitation Academy was now facing a monumental crisis; the inmates knew the fence was not "electrified." There was no holding us back now, and those poor nuns lost all control even though we knew Mother Superior still had her yardstick; that was no illusion, as Jack could only too well attest to.

Being the pathetic soul I was, it took me until third grade before I had built enough nerve to go past the hedge. Maybe the earth only opened some of the time, like that electric fence near our neighborhood.; all the other kids had touched it with no shock, but when I grabbed it ….

Most still believed there was a hell, but it was clear that these nuns did not have a secret portal located anywhere on the property. We soon questioned their every attempt to control us. If they had misled us once, then who knew? A little skepticism is a good starting point for learning, but not discipline.

That early bout of skepticism shaped me for years to come. I needed more than one's saying so to convince me of something. I decided soon after that there was no hell, but I hadn't needed that to keep me in line in those early years. By fourth grade, my parents had me enrolled in another school where the teachers went out for playground duty. Jack's fame gradually faded, and Susan soon found another classmate to worship. No one, however, will ever forget the day that Jack went to hell and back again.

TERROR ON THE THIRD FLOOR

I lay in my bed, trying hard to fall asleep. He would be coming soon, and I had to fall asleep before he came. Sweating profusely and turning from side to side, the harder I tried to doze, the more awake I was. This had happened every night for almost two weeks, and I was even more terrified tonight, knowing that he would indeed return. I assumed my night visitor was a "he," although I had no memory of the figure that attacked me every night because every child knew that monsters were always male. Alone on the third floor of a narrow row house in Baltimore, I enjoyed the independence and dealt with the array of monsters that frequented my room. Fortunately, I had an army of teddy bears guarding my room, and that night they were all in bed with me, buried deep under the covers. I was six now and supposed to be brave, but I was failing that test another night. Fuzzy, chief among the many bears, was tucked tightly under my arm, which gave me great comfort. At least I would not die alone. I listened for even the slightest indication that the visitor was coming. My bedroom was at the top of the stairs, and every sound was funneled up to my room.

I lived in a small tree-lined neighborhood nestled in a big, vibrant city. During the day, the traffic sounds, the frequent barking of an army of dogs, periodic shrieks of children playing in the street, and the muffled chatter of our neighbors just a wall away provided a constant backdrop. But at night, the house grew eerily quiet with one exception. The stairs creaked as the heat rose from the furnace in the basement. While my room was a couple of degrees short of Hell in the summer, I was the only warm one in the house in winter. When the furnace came on, the old wooden stairs would start to creak as they expanded, and the creaking would gradually ascend as the warming made its way up to the third floor. I, however, could easily differentiate the creaking from actual footsteps.

My parents slept in the bedroom below, and I would often hear one of them walk out in the hall and down the stairs before returning shortly with whatever they were retrieving, either the jiggling of ice in a glass of water or the clatter of a spoon in a bowl if my mother were sneaking another bowl of ice cream up to her room. One had just returned from a trip to the first floor, and all was now silent in the house. It was when all quieted down that he would come. And he would come. He had for several weeks now. He would walk up the stairs and enter my room, stopping directly over my bed. He would bend over me, and I would start screaming, loud enough to bring my parents racing up the stairs. "It's just a dream," my mother would say, turning on the light to show me an empty room. But these were no dreams! Although the room might have been empty when my parents entered and turned on the light, he had been there. This was real!

In earlier years, I had experienced several incidents of night terror. Not the typical "bad dream," these were fits of sheer irrational terror, so consuming that I would still be screaming and shaking ten to fifteen minutes after awakening. The terror had always been precipitated by a small dream, which seemed incredibly silly when reason and rational thought returned, hardly the fodder of nightmares. On one occasion, my basketball rolled toward the staircase, and I could not stop it. In hindsight, it must have been both comical and incredibly perplexing to a parent trying to stop the hysteria of a child whose "basketball was rolling down the steps." My parents' attempts to restore reason and calm were ignored that night. On another occasion, my hysteria was punctuated by cries of, "I only have nine popsicle sticks, and I should have ten." My mother was a patient and loving soul, but dealing with this had not been covered in the Dr. Spock book that every parent in the 1950s used as their bible.

These recent visits had touches of the night terror, but I honestly believed I had been awake the whole time despite my parents' futile attempts to convince me otherwise. After two weeks of these visits, I knew he would be coming again. I was completely awake now, and I could feel both Fuzzy under my arm and the other bears near me on the bed—even Chubby Tubby Timmy, the four-foot-tall bear I had just gotten for Christmas. I was ready, albeit frightened, for the next visit.

I kept telling myself I was awake, and Fuzzy assured me I was. We were all going to stay awake until he came. I was finally going to confront this nocturnal monster; this would be the showdown. A couple of weeks of terrifying encounters was enough. It would all end tonight.

The house was unusually silent now as the furnace had temporarily shut down, and I was listening for any sound that would tell me he was coming. Suddenly I heard the doorknob of our giant front door turn. This was it! Positive that I was awake, I squeezed Fuzzy a little tighter. The door opened and closed, and I waited. After what seemed an eternity, the first stair creaked under the weight of his foot as he began to ascend stairs. This was no creaking caused by rising heat, a more irregular pattern. Step after step creaked rhythmically as he ascended to the second floor. Each staircase had a turn near the top, and I could tell when he was making that turn. He was on the second floor now. Each of the previous nights, I had prayed that he would stop there and go no farther, but each night he headed up to the third floor. He seemed to have paused on the second floor, and I could only hope that tonight would be different—but I knew better.

I finally heard the first step on the next staircase creak, and I pulled Chubby Tubby Timmy close to me. The monster was moving slowly, almost seeming to pause on each step, or maybe time slowed down in my mind. But he was coming and soon reached the small landing where the steps turned. There was a light above this landing, and I could now see the figure's outline for the first time. Backlit, no details were visible, but this was a man, and he was almost to the third floor. With a couple more steps, he was on the floor and now turned toward my room. He remained a shadow as he approached the door and filled the whole doorway as he paused. I thought back to the previous nights when my parents had insisted that I was asleep. This was no dream! I could not have been more awake. I had to pretend to be asleep because everyone knew that monsters did not bother sleeping children, but curiosity kept me opening my eyes; I wanted to see at least who was going to kill me. I thought of screaming, but that would only bring my parents back up to, once again, tell me that it was all just a dream.

The figure approached the bed, and I could hear him breathing. One does not hear someone breathing in a dream. This was all too real, and I could even feel Fuzzy trembling under my arm. Chubby Tubby Timmy had even retreated under the covers. The man was beside the bed now, but I could still not see who was about to attack me. Too terrified to move, I saw him beginning to bend over me. He was reaching down now, and I waited for his hands to grab my throat. I had to get under the covers, but it was too late. Surprisingly, his hands gripped the blankets and pulled them up over Fuzzy and me. "Goodnight, George," came from a familiar voice, and I opened my eyes to see my father. The stranger never returned ever again.

Return From the Dark Side

I once led a life of crime. A hardened criminal, I was regularly stealing and even robbed one house. Beginning with minor thefts, as I got bolder, I moved up to larger and larger jobs until I was finally apprehended, tried, and found guilty. Greed drove me to do things I normally never would have stooped to do, and I did learn my lesson. I was seven years old.

Age seven is supposed to be the Age of Reason, when one should know the difference between right and wrong. I both knew and ignored the difference. Money was power, and my ten-cent allowance didn't stretch that far. I don't know what possessed me to pick up that penny off my mother's dressing table, but it was easy to rationalize that she would never miss it—and she didn't. A penny was significant when a candy bar or a pack of baseball cards cost just five cents. I remember thinking how easy it was to pull off the "job." As chaotic as my mother's purse was, I knew there had to be more of them floating around at the bottom of that organized mess. She always carried a large purse that served several purposes. With three young children at that time, she always needed a supply of tissue, toys to amuse a bored child while out, snacks, a book to read, and enough make-up to prepare the entire cast of Cats. She, a child of the Depression, wasted nothing, and on many occasions, while out for a meal, she would ask a server for more dinner rolls, which were tossed right into that bottomless purse. If stranded on a desert island, she could have survived an eternity. The change would often just be thrown into the purse, and she would frequently cause a major checkout line back-up as she fished around in that sack for the necessary change. Disorganized but ever so resourceful. If you needed something, she could retrieve it from that purse. My thoughts now went to the change she would never miss.

I was soon retrieving a penny periodically and, growing bolder, eventually went for nickels and dimes. As the weeks passed, my baseball card collection started to grow. I felt guilty when Saturday came, and Dad gave me my dime allowance. That's where I made the first of many mistakes, telling him one Saturday that he could keep the dime if he were short of cash. What seemed like an impressive comment had to sound utterly moronic to an intelligent man, a trial lawyer by trade. What seven-year-old kid turns down their allowance?

At the time, I was in second grade at a local Catholic school taught by cloistered nuns. I must have slept through the class on the seventh commandment, "Thou shalt not steal." Well-schooled in the fires of Hell, I can't remember how I rationalized my actions, but something I did in school must have eased some guilt. The nuns were always pumping their array of charities and continually asked the kids to get money from their parents to donate. Sister had a cabinet full of toys one could choose from after donating a certain amount, and this had our band of Catholic warriors bringing in a steady stream of cash to help her empty this toy cabinet. While some of the kids were bringing in enough money regularly to continue getting "prizes" from the top shelf, the little I brought in only got me things from the bottom shelf, primarily just holy cards (pictures of the Big Guy and all the saints). For this seven-year-old, a rookie card of St. Thomas Aquinas just didn't cut the mustard (I never understood why one had to 'cut' mustard); the saints couldn't even play baseball, and they were all dead! No one would trade a Hank Aaron card for a Thomas Aquinas rookie. That's when some of my ill-gotten gains started heading toward the Catholic Church. I remember the day I got a little puzzle (the one where you must roll all the little balls each into its hole) off the shelf above the bottom. Sister also kept a chart of how much each kid donated, and soon I was not at the very bottom of the list.

Granted, Dad was a lawyer, but the pay was minimal early in his career, and my sister was already incurring significant medical bills. Mom felt her regular Sunday collection donation was all we could spare, but I was fixated on that chart and the airplane models on that top shelf. My desire to go for the gold, combined with my increasing boldness, led my thievery to a higher level, and then came that day I lifted a one-dollar bill from Mom's purse. Oh, did that ever feel good. Although only seven, I had already worked out my line of defense in the unlikely event that I was to get caught. I was collecting money for those poor starving children in other lands—and taking a small cut off the side for my efforts. The CEOs of charities got paid, didn't they? Additionally, I thought my father, the lawyer, would be proud of the detailed argument I was prepared to present. Momentum was now carrying me downhill in a hurry.

Then came the night of the fateful cocktail party that my parents hosted. Mom and Dad always needed to entertain, and their cocktail parties often became raucous events, although civility reigned. The conversation would grow louder, and the jokes more off-color, directly proportional to the amount of alcohol consumed. This was only a decade after many had served in World War II, and I can understand why alcohol attained a higher status than it did in my generation. This occurred during the Golden Age of Hollywood, where cigarette smoking was universal, and every movie contained multiple "Can I offer you a drink?" lines. While my parents were not heavy drinkers, their cocktail hour always saw them each having two drinks. Well into this party, there was no hiding from the excessive noise, even upstairs.

I put my sister and brother to bed, knowing that, as the eldest, I could stay up an extra half hour. I went into the sitting room where I had left a couple of toys, and that's where I encountered the mother lode—the giant pile of coats left by the guests—and all their PURS-ES. You can easily guess the rest. Knowing I could hear footsteps coming up the stairs, I started investigating each purse. Once again, thinking myself so very clever, I only took insignificant amounts from the handbags, knowing it wouldn't be missed, but I did well with twenty couples at the party. That following Monday, I made it to the top shelf.

There was an airplane model that I had been drooling over for weeks, and fortunately, none of the other kids had taken it. I present-ed my "donation" to the teacher first thing, and the model was mine. Sister then told the class I had brought in the most significant single amount for the year. I was a celebrity now!

Time passed, and my life of crime continued. I often wonder why my parents never asked how I was suddenly coming home with mod-els, religious statues, and other trinkets. It all made me bolder and bolder; I was now a hardened criminal. In hindsight, however, Dad was on to me, and he would soon bring the house I had built down on me. I even started taking from a neighbor's purse when at their home. Life was great, the Church was thriving, and my baseball card collection was growing.

Then came the fateful day I should have realized would eventu-ally come. Dad always laid out his change on his bureau at the end of each day, and I finally got the nerve to remove a coin or two. I had been hesitant to take any of this treasure since it was all visible, unlike in a purse; it would be much easier to see if a coin or two were missing. However, some days, there was quite a pile there, and I determined a missing coin would go unnoticed. This day, a shiny fifty-cent piece was sitting in the pile of change, and I couldn't re-sist. Into my pocket it went. A few minutes later, I heard my father's footsteps as he came up to my third-floor room. Somehow, I knew what was about to happen.

"George, have you by any chance seen that fifty-cent piece that was on my bureau?"

"No, Dad, why do you ask?"

"It seems to have just disappeared. You don't by any chance have a fifty-cent piece, do you?"

Deciding to be super cool, I told him I had one, but it certainly wasn't his coin. It was the change I had gotten at the local drugstore. I had forgotten that my father was a trial attorney, and I soon was being questioned in excruciating detail. What had I bought that would have resulted in fifty cents change? Where had I gotten the dollar I used for the purchase? And the questioning continued. I was proud of myself as I confidently fielded question after question, thinking I would walk away from this smelling like a rose. Then came the question I never anticipated …

"What's the date on that coin?"

The question alone floored me, and I lost all composure, stumbling and bumbling as I told Dad that no one looked at the dates on their coins. I thought I had weathered this bomb until he said, "My coin was dated '1954', and it had a little scratch just above the date. Can I see your coin?"

The amazing thing was that he had never once accused me of taking the coin. In hindsight, he had tripped me up multiple times with his questioning, but I now knew the game was over. I couldn't refuse to show him the coin, but I would be toast if he saw it. I then realized this had all been a setup. The crime spree was over.

I had prepared an extravagantly detailed explanation for the events of the last several months, but something told me that I had already dug a deep enough hole. What a relief to finally confess to all. I thought about just admitting to the fifty-cent piece theft, but, although only seven, something told me that Dad knew more than he was letting on. Within a half hour, I had confessed to all, making sure to let him know how much of it had gone to charity. He left me alone in the room while he decided on an appropriate punishment. That was the most prolonged two hours of my life.

Shockingly, he never got mad. Dad always knew that psychological torture was the worst punishment and that the long wait was painful. There were to be consequences, however. I would lose my allowance for an extended period, have to confront the next-door mom, confess my taking from her purse, and get the belt. I balked at facing the neighbor and was told I would remain in my room until I chose to do so. It was late that day, and I decided to wait until morning … I certainly wouldn't want to disturb a neighbor late in the day. The psychological torture continued. It was an exceptionally long evening and night.

Amazingly nothing was said over breakfast; nothing needed to be said as I was doing a severe number on myself. Knocking on the neighbor's door was terrifying, but I assume from her reaction that Dad had clued her in. She was so nice about it, once again sensing I was well into remorse at this point. Then it was home for the "beating." I've never been a fan of corporal punishment, but I deserved it. A parent striking a child in a fit of rage is one thing, but my ultra-controlled father was quite the opposite. He sent me to my room to await the punishment, giving me enough time to sweat it out. I could hear my mother downstairs imploring him to go easy on me, but I wasn't worried about pain. Nothing hurt more than knowing I had let them down. He finally came upstairs, took off his belt, asked me to bend over, and that's all I remember. If there was any pain associated with the lashing, I was not aware of it. He said nothing; it was all just a simple emotionless business deal. Nothing more was ever said.

I can't say I made it the next 62 years without ever taking anything; I was not the perfect child, but that period stayed with me. Yes, I do take soap from motel rooms. And while no parent is perfect, my father shone brightly that day. He never raised his voice once. He may have been disappointed in my actions, but he never lost faith in me.

I also learned very quickly not to mess with a father who was a trial attorney. I saw him once let a witness "hang himself" on the witness stand, as most guilty people will do, given enough time. And did I ever hang myself that day! I still marvel at the incredible self-control he exhibited. My boys will tell you readily that I often failed in this area. I almost wish he had gotten mad; I more than deserved it. What his remarkable business-like self-control did, however, was double my remorse. He provided no target for argument or reaction; he just let me stew in my juices. The Catholic Church got to keep all their illicit donations, and I've often felt like the donation reward system was an invitation for a young kid to cross a line. No excuses here; I would have found another reason to go over to the Dark Side. I've never had reason to get on a courtroom witness stand, but if I ever did, I would scream "GUILTY" before ever having to endure that psychological torture again.

God is a No Show

Being a five-year-old is challenging work, and, watching my grandchildren, they are doing a far better job weathering the storm than I did. Kindergarten left no impression on me whatsoever. My parents told me how bright I was, but then parents tell every kid that. With all the things kids do in kindergarten, I only have retained one pathetic memory. I played St. Joseph in the school play, but even most of that has long been erased from my memory. I'm sure we went on field trips, but I remember none; no memories of painting, learning the alphabet, or even lunch. The only memory was an unhappy and stressful one—eating lollipops. OK, I do like lollipops or did like them, but there's far more to the memory than that. We were given a lollipop after lunch and before rest time, and we had to finish the lollipop before lying down to pretend to sleep because everyone knows that a room full of five-year-old children are not going to sleep. But I couldn't finish the lollipop before the call to rest was given. This was highly stressful. I was supposed to lie down, but I still had a lollipop.

Being a shy five-year-old, the solution was simple; hide the remaining lollipop under the carpet. Why a five-year-old would stress over this is beyond explanation. Sadly, it was traumatic enough that I remember this vividly, playing out every day after lunch. My parents paid for an entire year of kindergarten instruction, and I only remember hiding grape lollipops under the school carpet. Years later, I felt sorry for the poor school custodian. The point that all this mindless meandering leads to is that five and six-year old's sometimes have a warped view of how the world works. They also take things literally, a fact which has gotten many a parent in trouble.

With my lack of progress in kindergarten and traumatic experiences with lollipops, my parents needed to salvage what was left of their first child, so off I went to a parochial school. This must have been a much happier experience as there were no lollipops and rest time. We had to do this thing called "work." With that massive lollipop roadblock out of the way, the door was thrust open for me to ascend the tower of knowledge. However, I chose the wrong door. I'm sure I was taught to read, write, and do arithmetic, but I have no memories of this, at least in first grade. However, it was here that this abnormal mound of DNA was to become derailed for a lifetime, suffering a disappointment that still reverberates today.

The school had a principal, but we soon learned that the absolute authority in the school was the big JC himself. I had been dragged to church and indoctrinated into the existence of a supreme being, so I knew the drill. The nuns gave us a twenty-five-page catechism, which we had to memorize from cover to cover.

> Q. What effect had the sin of Adam on all mankind?
> A. All mankind is born in a state of sin and misery.
>
> Q. What is that sinful nature which we inherit from Adam called?
> A. Original sin.
>
> Q. What does every sin deserve?
> A. The wrath and curse of God.

I hate to disappoint religious educators (yes, these catechismal torture devices still exist), but this doesn't register with a six-year-old child. I lived in the concrete world of ice cream, presents, baseball, and … lollipops. We memorized and recited, never understanding one word we were saying, and considering that I was "born in a state of sin and misery" deserving "the wrath and curse of God," that was probably a good thing. However, I did understand one part quite well:

Q. Where is God?
A. God is everywhere.

Q. Can you see God?
A. No; I cannot see God, but he always sees me.*

It was a little unnerving to know that God was following me everywhere with a scorecard, which had to be pretty well packed by this point … at least ten pages of "stuck another lollipop under the carpet today." And it bothered me that he was even watching while I was sitting on a toilet. Was there no privacy? However, the real bummer was that I couldn't see him. (I remember wondering how we knew God was a "him" if we couldn't see him.) Then came the day when Sister told us that we were going to church the next day and would SEE GOD. I remembered back to the catechism telling us we could not see God, and here she was telling us we would tomorrow, in fact, see the Almighty himself. We'd been told that the catechism contained only truths, but this sure sounded like a lie. Howard must have been on the same wavelength because he raised his hand and pointed out the apparent discrepancy. Sister once again said we would see God in all his glory the next day. Wow, I decided that first grade was one cool place to be.

That evening and well into the night, my mind went into overdrive. What would this guy look like? He had to be extremely old since he got the earthly ball rolling. Since the word "he" was always used to refer to the Almighty, it would be a man, and, of course, he would be white; I remember wondering if Black folks minded God being a different color. Several years later, I learned humans had orig-

---

* Reformed.org, "Historic Church Documents: The Children's Catechism," https://reformed.org/historic-confessions/the-childrens-catechism/

inated in Africa, and since we were "created in his image," I then decided God was an old black guy. My sister, wise for her age, said God was a woman because that would make "her" kinder and more intelligent. He had to be huge to be everywhere at once, but how would he fit in our school if he were that big? An omnipresent God certainly couldn't fit through the door to the school, and if he were in our school, how could he be watching everyone else in the world? Would he be wearing golden robes and hurling lightning bolts? The school was boring enough that I relished the thought of a good fireworks show inside. And how had Sister known where to send the invitation? What happened if he forgot or, more likely, had to respond to an emergency somewhere else?

I could hardly sleep that night and kept imagining how the next day would play out. I beat everyone to breakfast the next morning, even after taking more time than usual to get dressed. I wanted to make a great first impression, especially after all those lollipop incidents the year before. My whole life had led to this moment, and all those grueling hours memorizing the catechism seemed worth it. I was ready to make a big impression if he asked me to recite a passage or two. Finally, I had a chance to redeem myself.

Arriving at school that morning, several of my classmates reacted similarly; this would be a day to remember. Only Susan, whose mother had told her that she wasn't going to see God, seemed subdued, but we quickly reminded her that nuns could not lie; it's in their contract when they sign. Susan was soon back on board. The moment Sister walked into the room, she was immediately hit with the question of "when" the big moment would occur. She informed us that we would be going to Mass, and after prayer and blessing, the priest would "unveil" him. Wow! Were they ever building up the suspense! And that would have to be one immense veil to cover up the omnipresent Almighty. And since he could see all, why would he be covered with a veil anyway?

We could hardly contain ourselves that morning. Who wants to read or do arithmetic when we were getting ready to see the Big Guy himself? Even the most mischievous among us were on good behavior that morning, but that was the longest morning of my life. Too much suspense! We went through the catechism one more time; we all excelled except for Howard, but we had already decided he was going to Hell anyway. He had snuck a toy into Mass the other day and was not caught. We all figured God was worn out from continually updating Howard's scorecard.

Finally, the time came for us to line up and march down to the school chapel. I'm not sure what I expected to find, but nothing seemed different when we rounded the corner to enter the chapel. I was hoping to see this massive veil with God underneath impatiently waiting to pop out, and I wasn't the only one surprised and disappointed as one of my classmates called out, "Where is he?" After an emphatic "shhh" from Sister, she quietly pointed to a small, veiled structure, about 2 feet tall, sitting on the side of the altar. "In there," Sister said. Excitement quickly evolved into confusion. "God was a midget!" In all my mental reconstructions in the last twenty-four hours, I had never pictured God that way. Maybe he was a leprechaun; they were magical, weren't they? But how could a little guy be omnipotent, whatever that meant? Worse still, we would have to wait until most of the way through the Mass to see the "Little Guy." As I sat there, I deduced that the Son of God must have been a midget also, but the pictures always portrayed him as a standard size. Things didn't add up no matter how I thought the issue through.

The service consistently defied the normal passage of time, but the clock went backward that day. The Mass was in Latin, which meant it made about as much sense as the catechism. I kept watching the veil to see if it moved. There was no movement, but then God must be talented enough to be able to stand still—a feat unknown to me. God was a busy guy; why were they making him wait so long for his grand appearance? How ridiculous it was to make the Almighty not only wait but have to hide under a veil. However, the time finally arrived, and suddenly the priest was reaching up to pull off the veil. We all edge forward in our seats, holding our collective breath and trying to get the best look possible. Off the veil came, and there was … nothing! What they call a monstrance was sitting on the altar; we had seen one of these before. Several students murmured, "Where is he?" Sister quickly whispered that the priest had to put him in the structure now sitting on the altar. He opened a little circular glass door on the golden, bejeweled structure and then went to retrieve another object. This was getting more bizarre by the minute because now I realized that God was even tinier than I expected—no immense ruler adorned in a crown and flowing robes, for sure.

The priest returned with a small container, which he opened. Out came a large white circular host. Wait a minute! I had seen these many times before, at every Mass, in fact! We had been tricked, and disappointment was about to evolve into anger when I heard Sister whisper that the priest had to bless it first. Magic! All right, now we were getting somewhere. The priest would utter some incantation, and the Big Guy, or Little Guy, would appear out of a puff of smoke. He needed a grand entrance, which was where this was all headed. The priest lapsed into a round of prayers in Latin, and I kept waiting for the inevitable "Hocus Pocus," which never came. We had been tricked! Only the host remained. I was crushed, disillusioned, and angry. What a horrible trick to play on a kid.

Back in the classroom, Sister would explain that God was there with us in the chapel, and we should have been able to see him "with our hearts." I wanted to tell her that the heart was not a sensory organ, that six-year-olds only see with their eyes; however, I could only sit there, confused and discouraged. We had been lied to, and I will never forget the disappointment I felt that day. I am no longer a practicing Catholic for several reasons; however, I don't blame Sister for that day. She believed and "saw" something that day, and I don't begrudge her the faith she had. My mind lives in a more factual, scientific world. However, looking back on that day, it was sad for young children to have their hopes dashed so completely by an innocent comment. Years later, I encountered a woman who claimed to have seen God, changing her life forever. I asked her what he looked like, but she really couldn't say. I asked her if he were a "white guy," but she could only say that what she saw defied description. If that helps her live a good life, more power to her, but that would hardly qualify as a good eyewitness account.

Children take things literally, a fact that adults often overlook, and many a child has jumped to the wrong conclusion by believing verbatim what passes out of an adult's mouth. My wife Jackie taught that age for years, and she knew this fact well. When one of her students was told that someone was "under the weather," he told another that this person must be "outside under the rain." I survived childhood, although many will say I never left it. It's surprising what silly things we often remember while so many of our experiences fade away quickly. I will never forget my disappointment that day, and I have to laugh when I remember that group of little children expecting to see the Almighty. What would I have done if he had appeared that day? What would I have said to him? It would have been a glorious day just as long as he hadn't offered me a lollipop!

SUMMER IN THE CITY

There was something special about summers in Baltimore for a child in the 1950s. While I live on a rural farm today, I grew up a child of the city. Both day and evening, the neighborhood would be alive with running and shouting children: skating, biking, and playing tag, stickball, dodge, and hopscotch on every available square yard of asphalt. Today, children retreat to their wired, air-conditioned caves, with a lucky few spending a couple of weeks at highly structured camps. We created our own adventure park with limited resources but unlimited imagination. While we might retreat indoors for a couple of hours in the middle of the day for a nap and reading, we charged back into the heat when given the signal. We created games, constantly evolving the rules, built forts and go-carts, explored what precious little natural space there was, and learned to compromise and adapt in our active social world. The afternoon games and activities were interrupted only by the tinkling of the bells of the Good Humor truck, which sent all racing home for change to buy ice cream or a popsicle. But at night the neighborhood really came alive as even parents bailed out of the oppressive heat inside for the gradually cooling night air.

We lived in a narrow three-story house on a tiny one-way street with a typical Baltimore alley running behind the house. Overshadowing us to the east was a monstrous apartment building. It wasn't until several years later that I discovered that the sun did rise before mid-morning. After ten in the summer, houses heated up like a furnace, driving us outside quickly. My third-floor bedroom quickly became an oven, and the only fan was in my parents' room on the second floor; air conditioning was a rare commodity at that time. By late evening, my room had cooled to 100 degrees, giving me another reason to argue with my parents when they called me in at night.

One advantage to living in a neighborhood with row houses was the army of kids to play and get into trouble with. We had two complete baseball teams just living on our little street. Baseball ruled in the 1950s, particularly since we were just a few blocks from Memorial Stadium, where the Baltimore Orioles and Colts played. We had a makeshift ballfield within walking distance, but the street we lived on was our primary playing field for daily stickball games.

Ball games consisted of either stickball or step ball. Step ball was played when there were insufficient players for an actual game. The concrete steps from the street up to the sidewalks provided a way to propel a hit. One player would throw the ball at the steps while the other player(s) were the fielders. Hitting the vertical surface of a step would create a ground ball, and hitting the angle could generate a fly ball. Rules always varied, but we spent many hours throwing a tennis ball or rubber ball against those steps.

The real excitement came when we could bring out enough friends for a game of stickball. A broom handle and tennis ball were all the equipment needed. A real bat and hard ball were saved for the big games which occurred on our makeshift ball field. The road we played stickball on ran uphill, adding an exciting dimension to our "field;" passed balls would roll all the way down the hill, sending the catcher sprinting down the road while all the runners could score. A long drive would eventually stop and roll back to the infield. We became quite adept at climbing over and under the parked cars to retrieve balls, while the runner was sprinting around the bases. Because the street was so narrow, the "field" was laterally compressed to a ridiculous extent, making it difficult to tell whether a runner was on first or third since the bases seemed to be side-by-side.

Evening posed another challenge to our ballgames, but the street-lights gave us a fighting chance. Watching the fielders racing around to find a ball they cannot see and the runners searching for the next base was always a comedy of errors. The challenge in playing street ball was to not hit the ball into Mrs. Cockman's yard since none of us had the nerve to cross her property line. We were all convinced that she had played the Wicked Witch of the West in the *Wizard of Oz* as she made Margaret Hamilton look like Marilyn Monroe. The poor soul sat in her living room, peering out the window, standing guard over her fifty square feet of yard, lest one of the "neighborhood delin-quents" try to trample her flowers. Landing a ball in her yard was an automatic home run and also an immediate end to the game unless we could find a second ball. Years later I felt so sorry for her, for she had to be the loneliest person on the planet. I often wish one of us had had the nerve to try to befriend her.

On special days, we would move to our "major league" field, Death Valley, as we called it. Right across from Johns Hopkins University was a small sandy lot in the shadow of a tall apartment building. The field was wide enough to put in a baseball diamond that was properly sized, with no first and third basemen standing side-by-side, and it was LEVEL. There was one minor drawback; the wall bounding the apartment building was only about 100 feet from home plate. There was no room for an outfield, but then the wall was thirty feet high. The outfielders sometimes had to play inside the infielders to retrieve the fly balls which caromed off the wall. A shot over the wall was a home run, but unfortunately would end the game; however, this rare-ly happened. We spent many afternoons baking in that little sandy corner that never had a breeze, hence its name!

Biking, roller skating, and driving homemade go-carts were daily activities. We were always trying to make the best go-cart, which nev-er consisted of more than a couple of boards nailed together on top of three or four roller skates. That was our domain; fathers were not allowed to help. Each time we were motivated to build the best cart ever, and after hours of pathetic banging away, we'd produce something that looked just like the one we had made the day before. No matter: it was our best ever. Biking was limited to our street and the one that paralleled it, but we had ways of making it exciting. Baseball cards, although playing cards were better, attached to the wheel framework with a clothespin, created a great sound as the spokes hit the card. Racing down the road with our bikes sputtering away, we were kings of the road. My parents always wondered why their card decks never had fifty-two cards.

My biking career began on my seventh birthday when I got my first bicycle. A gift from my grandmother, it was a slick red bike with training wheels. That afternoon, my father took me out into the alley for the inaugural ride. Rarely did a car venture up the alley; so, this seemed like the ideal place to get started. With one small push, Dad sent me off down the hill. This was in the days when no one had ever heard of a bike helmet or knee/elbow pads. I sailed down the hill, exhilarated and only faintly aware of my father screaming behind me. As I neared the bottom of the hill, I finally figured out the reason for his screams; he had omitted one small detail from Bicycling 101 ... how to stop! Dad had tried desperately to keep up with me, but his sprinting made his pleas to me almost incoherent. At the bottom of the hill was a busy street with two-way traffic, and I was still gaining speed. This was before bikes had hand brakes, and it never occurred to me to reverse the rotation of the pedals. Being the genius that I was, it never even occurred to me to stop peddling. As I neared 39th Street, I could see the heavy traffic, and I tensed for the imminent impact. I sailed out into the road, somehow dodging both lanes of traffic, and that's when things went from bad to worse.

My father had been left far behind at this point, and he undoubtedly was trying to figure out how to explain to my mother that they had one less child. I had been so concerned with avoiding cars that

I had failed to consider what was past the cars. I hit the curb on the other side of the road moving full speed and went airborne, my fall being broken by … a rose bush. I don't remember how long it took for my father and a kind bystander to disentangle me and my bike. I remember the pain and the blood, but I also remember my father carefully explaining to me at this point how the brakes worked. Ah yes, the joys of the city.

No child in the neighborhood had much spending money. With luck, we could get a few cents shoveling snow in the winter, but in the summer, money was scarce. Not only were there basically no lawns to cut, but there were twenty of us available to cut the two lawns that did exist. We did have a small side yard that was just wide enough to put in a swing set. To say that we could cut the grass with a pair of scissors was not that much of an exaggeration. But there was "gold in them thar hills" … trash. This was the era of deposit glass bottles; plastic thankfully was a rare commodity. A 6.5 oz. bottle of coke cost five cents, but one had to pay a one-cent deposit on it. As today, many humans could never find a trash can, and certainly not a store to return it. A penny to a seven-year-old kid was a small fortune. Every morning I'd take off with my little red wagon in search of gold; one quickly learned to get out early to beat the rush. On a good day, you might find close to a dozen bottles, but ten cents could buy two packs of baseball cards at the gift shop in the nearby apartment building. I'd leave the store and plop down on the curb to open the packs, the goal always being to find an Oriole card. Cards came out in series then, and it was always exciting when we realized that we were digging into another series of cards, with the prospect of getting new Orioles.

All the neighborhood kids collected and traded them. I could collect my heroes, arranging them and rearranging them on a regular basis. Bound with rubber bands and kept in a shoe box, this was my treasure trove. Whenever visiting a friend, that shoe box always went with me. In those days, they were collected just for fun; no one ever thought about condition or their value as an investment. I specifically remember trading away any Mickey Mantle card I got; to possess a Yankee card in our neighborhood was like being cursed with the Black Spot. There was no hesitation then to trading my 1956 Mantle (current value: $1500) for a card of Willy Miranda (current value: $12), the Orioles shortstop. My parents eventually threw out my card collection, thousands of dollars now down the drain. But then if no cards had been discarded, they would be worth far less today. I'm sure mine were in fair to poor condition anyway from the constant handling. Additionally, bundling with rubber bands and attaching them to our bikes mostly did mine in.

Nighttime was when our neighborhood came alive. The smell of a barbecue drifting up and down the street sent all in search of a free hot dog, Ball games, hopscotch, and an occasional "capture the flag" game kept all the children busy, but the real fun began when the fireflies, "lightning bugs," came out. That was the ultimate sport: dodging cars, trees, and thorn bushes in pursuit of one of these critters, only visible when lit up. This was sport enough as it was, but the fact that Johns Hopkins would pay money for live fireflies fueled our engines. The University was researching how to create light without heat (glow sticks were the first byproduct of this) and knew that local kids could provide them with their specimens. To be truthful, our fireflies rarely made it to Hopkins and usually didn't make it to the next morning. But we were determined to get rich ... more baseball cards.

We were always allowed to stay out late; safety was really not a concern. There was safety in numbers, and did we ever have numbers! It was also a different time; I'm sure there was some crime, but we were not aware of it. But nighttime for us was the best playtime of all. There was so much asphalt around that things cooled slowly; you could cook an egg on the street in the heat of the day. However, when the sun was gone, a breeze started drifting through the neighborhood. The insides of the houses were still ovens and would not start to cool down until midnight. Many a night I remember staying out until ten or eleven; few would allow that today. When I finally did go in, going to sleep was an impossibility. Within minutes my sheets were soaked, and sleep was not even close to happening. I'd listen to the sounds of the city: the car horns, the occasional fire engine rolling down 39th St., dogs barking, and the arguing in the house adjoining ours. I would reflect on an exciting day and make big plans for the next day, and sleep would soon overtake me.

It was a wonderful time to be a child, and although I would never live in a city now, I remember those days as being the best ... no homework, wonderful companionship, and freedom. It was, in many ways, the ultimate classroom where we learned diplomacy, how to amuse ourselves, to use limited resources to creatively invent, and the skill of bartering. We knew and cared for our neighbors. Few had televisions, and the heat forced us to interact with our neighbors. Winter might see us retreat to our houses, but summer was when a neighborhood came alive, and we became rulers of our universe.

THE RETURN OF
BONNIE AND CLYDE

The two sat on their bikes, looking down at the course they were going to run. Bill was nervous and wanted to back out, but Gussie would not let him. She was fearless and seemed oblivious to the potential disaster if they failed to make the run. The younger Bill looked down at the course and saw no way that they could succeed. Gussie said, "We're going on the count of three. I'll go first, and then you follow right behind." Bill protested one more time, but Gussie was already starting to count.

"One." She tensed her body in anticipation of the steep descent.

"Two." She started to lean forward.

"Three." With that, she launched her tricycle down the steep staircase, with Bill starting soon after. Bouncing down step after step, she somehow managed to stay on the tricycle while Bill lurched sideways and capsized almost immediately. He and his tricycle began crashing together down the stairs. His screams mixed with an incredible crash as Gussie somehow made it to the bottom of the stairs before crashing into a hall table. The table's leaf, which had laid vertically against the wall, came crashing down, knocking over a glass lamp, several figurines, and a china vase complete with flowers.

My parents sprinted into the hallway upon hearing the screams and accompanying noise and saw the devastation. Their three-year-old son lay on the steps crying while his tricycle lay with the table, lamp, and vase wreckage. Their five-year-old daughter sat proudly on her upright bike, completely unhurt. "Mom and Dad, I did it."

Thus began a reign of terror that would rival the run of Bonnie and Clyde.

❖ ❖ ❖

Gussie was eighteen months younger than me and as different from me as anyone. She was fearless, daring, and usually confrontational, while I was the shy, well-behaved older sibling (trans: I was boring). In those early years, she was constantly being compared to me by my parents in an attempt to steer her toward the right path. Always in trouble, it had to be difficult for her to hear this. However, there was a biological reason for her behavior. Because of a significant congenital circulatory issue, she was in pain every day of her life.

Unfortunately, in those early years of her life, she was merely thought of as a mischievous child. She was loved by all, and as incorrigible as she could be at times, she was a remarkably loving and caring child. She would also later be diagnosed as manic-depressive, and those manic periods were classic. In later years, medication would be available, which could minimize the extremes we saw early in her life.

Her accomplice in crime was our brother Bill, two and a half years younger than her, with his own fun-loving, playful streak. He adored his older sister, but it was impossible not to like Gussie. Her infectious laughter could brighten any day. Bill was treated as the baby of the three of us and played the role to the hilt. He didn't talk when most his age did and did not take his first step until he was twenty-one months. Why walk if everyone is waiting on you and getting things for you? When the three of us were young, Gussie and Bill were a team, and I played the role of the well-behaved older brother. Gussie could talk the stripes off of a tiger, and Bill was her willing partner in crime. In truth, I was often jealous of all the fun these two had, fun which started my parents' hair turning gray.

The two of them could get in trouble faster than anyone alive; Dennis the Menace must have taken lessons from them. There was the time they overflowed three toilets on the same day or the day they decided to paint the wallpaper in our front hallway with paint they found in my father's tool shed. My amazingly cool father, the lawyer, completely lost all composure the day he opened his briefcase and discovered that vitally important legal documents had all been beautifully colored with crayons. Dad failed to see any humor in that situation, and I'm not sure the judge appreciated getting the pink and purple deposition the next day. However, the legal world does need to take itself a little less seriously.

The two of them were carried to the emergency room enough times that they must have had honorary plaques on the hospital wall, and our wonderful family doctor spent as much time with them as anyone. He made enough visits to our home that he and my parents became close personal friends.

One day, in particular, was most memorable. My mother was a caring and vigilant parent, but a few seconds was all that Gussie needed to launch into one of her escapades. I remember walking into the living room just as Gussie was leaving. Bill, three at the time, sat on the floor, looking his usual happy and carefree self. There was never a happier child. I was carrying a box of my treasured baseball cards to sort when I noticed a giant bubble launching from his mouth. Blowing bubbles was a routine activity in our house but done outside, and Bill had no container of soap bubbles or wand. His next exhalation produced another bubble, and this continued. Asking him what he was doing got no response, and I was impressed that he had developed this exceptional talent. As my mother walked into the room, her response was quite different.

"Bill, what did you do?" He only smiled.

"Did you eat something?"

"Candy."

Mom immediately called for my sister, who undoubtedly had played some part in this. Gussie walked into the room and admitted she had given him the candy after first denying any involvement. I immediately wanted to get some of this candy as I had no luck blowing bubbles with gum, and this was better than bubble gum as it led to one emitting what looked like soap bubbles with every breath. After some serious interrogation, Gussie was sent to get the "candy," returning shortly with a box of mothballs. That's when Mom let loose one of her patented screams. I always felt sorry for our neighbors, just a thin wall away from the adjacent row house. They must have often wondered what was going on in our remarkable home.

Gussie admitted to talking him into eating the mothballs, and he had consumed a good portion of the box's contents. There is little exaggeration here when I say Gussie could talk the stripes off of a tiger. To this day, I wonder how she could have talked Bill into eating one mothball, but a sizable number of them? Mothballs contain naphthalene which gives off a powerful and pungent odor. They're so potent that even a minute fragment is easily detected. How Bill got the first mothball close to his mouth is amazing, but eat it … and then a second … and more! Bill quickly went from a bubble machine to a lethargic camper, and the whole family piled in the car to head to the nearest emergency room. The doctors in the emergency room had never heard of anyone eating more than one mothball. If anyone needed evidence of Gussie's powers of persuasion, this was exhibit A thru Z.

Naphthalene is dangerous because it kills red blood cells needed for carrying oxygen, which would explain why Bill became quite lethargic. In the emergency room, they pumped out the contents of his stomach, and he suffered no long-term effects. Fortunately for Gussie, everyone focused so much on Bill that they had forgotten who fed him the mothballs. However, this was just a warm-up for Gussie's pièce de résistance.

Several months later, my parents hosted a large party that would take a most interesting twist. My parents' parties were epic as they had many colorful and boisterous friends. After a couple of rounds of drinks, the volume of the laughter would increase, and the men would start singing one college song after another. This particular party, however, was to be a more formal affair as it was partly related to Dad's legal practice, and all came dressed as if attending a ball. Mom had hired kitchen help, but I was to watch my three younger siblings. Kim was still an infant, and my attention was primarily devoted to her. If I could get her asleep, I could keep Gussie and Bill entertained.

To this day, I have no idea how Gussie organized the event that was about to occur. The street we lived on was densely populated, especially with children Bill's age, four. Somehow Gussie was able to get four of these little boys into our house and upstairs. I missed this whole maneuver as I was rocking Kim to sleep. I soon headed downstairs, unaware of the group now assembled in Bill's room. Wandering through the party, I found it much quieter and more dignified than usual. Blending into the crowd, I began filling up on hors d'oeuvres. I was downing my fiftieth mini weenie when I heard the scream. Then another … and another. Had someone seen a mouse? Moving into the next room, I immediately saw the cause of the screams. Racing from room to room were five completely naked little boys. I caught a glance at my mother, whose look was way beyond horrified. After circling twice through all the rooms, they headed up the stairs passing the individual who undoubtedly orchestrated the event, Gussie.

While several women were still showing complete disgust, several men were chuckling, and the general noise level of the party doubled. I never found out if Gussie got in trouble; with her track record for impishness, this was just chalked up as another indiscretion. For me, it absolutely made the party. I have no idea what possessed her to pull off this stunt. Several elderly women may have been permanently traumatized, but Gussie certainly livened up that party.

Gussie, never one for subtlety, loved to test a potential friend to see if they were worthy of her time. She may have lost a few potential friends with this procedure, but the friends she developed were true friends. My wife, Jackie, was subjected to this initiation on her first visit to the family farm. Gussie invited Jackie for a short sail on our simple sailfish. Sailing to a shallow spot where Gussie knew the bottom to be extremely muddy, she flipped the sailfish over, dumping my future wife into knee-deep mud. The two quickly giggled as they wallowed in the deep mud, and Gussie officially accepted Jackie into the family.

Tragically her stunts would become darker and more troubled as she reached her teen years, and she would first run away from home at age thirteen. She was institutionalized several times until the doctors finally treated her manic-depressive disorder with lithium. The exploits of our family's Bonnie and Clyde became a thing of the past, and I missed their harmless antics. Bill would continue the tradition to a certain extent, becoming our own nature boy, collecting every wild organism he could get his hands on. The window wells of our house were overpopulated with box turtles, and he probably single-handedly led to their decline. His favorite pet was Izzy, a de-scented skunk, with whom he would terrorize our neighborhood while walking with it on a leash. Watching pedestrians suddenly cross the street as Bill and Izzy approached was always fun.

In hindsight, it was difficult seeing Bill lose the good times that he and Gussie had as her troubles accumulated. She remained the warm, fun-loving person she was, but her bouts of depression would take her away from us. Many of her friends bailed on her, but those closest to her knew her to be the same individual as before. What was lost was the remarkable teamwork of this dynamic duo.

It was both fitting and tragic that they would spend their last couple of days together. Bill, engaged, and Gussie, married, would both attend a close friend's wedding in 1982, dying in a car accident on the way home. Bill had become an award-winning journalist, and Gussie, still saddled with major medical issues, was finally overcoming many of her psychological problems. While both grown adults, they still retained their marvelously mischievous side, but sadly Bonnie and Clyde would never ride again.

The Culinary House of Horrors

My mother was a wonderful, caring mother, a real saint, and I couldn't have asked for a more loving one. However, she checked her halo at the door when she entered the kitchen. There is not nor ever will be a plaque for her in the hallowed Culinary Hall of Fame. Betty Crocker and Julia Childs would never have dared enter our kitchen, more of a House of Horrors. I don't know whether she ever could cook, but I know her mother could; my grandmother's southern-style breakfasts were feasts fit for royalty. Mom was the oldest of four girls, and it would seem logical during the period in which she grew up that she would have been schooled in the culinary arts. Women then were often educated to be good wives, and cooking ability was integral to that resume. Mom must have slept through that class.

We were not poor, and Mom had the resources to purchase the necessary ingredients for a meal; it's just that not much happened between the store and the table. As I was told, my mother's cooking career got off to a horrific start. My parents' first meal in their new home consisted of Mom's attempt to cook a lobster. The lobster won! The next night was her first attempt to bake something. A slight burn ended this operation, and when she finally remembered that there was something in the oven, an autopsy failed to identify it. Day three sealed her fate and ended any hope of our family ever getting a gourmet meal. At ten in the morning, a mouse ran across the floor as she was about to start cooking a masterpiece for her new husband. Mom was still outside in the car when Dad got home, and they went out for dinner that night.

It is safe to say that Mom never attempted baking after that day. I have no memory of her baking bread, cake, or cookies in my lifetime. She did once try baking cookies from a purchased roll of dough. The only problem is that she chose to do this on a day when I had the worst digestive ailment I can ever remember. It was a day when I ran a fever and spent the better part of the day sitting on the bathroom floor, hugging the toilet. Nothing was heading down my esophagus without making a round trip. I had reached a point in the early afternoon when my stomach had been emptied several times over. That's when the odor of these baking refrigerator cookies started drifting up the stairs and into my room, sending me running to the commode all afternoon. She even came up later in the day and offered me a couple of cookies, and I know I was rude as I raced again for the bathroom. To this day, the smell of those particular cookies causes an instantaneous digestive aversion.

Mom's cooking wasn't bad; it was essentially nonexistent. Fry a piece of meat in a pan, open a can of vegetables, and prepare her pièce de résistance, Jell-O. Starchy vegetables usually consisted of instant mashed potatoes from a box or undercooked Minute Rice. She had meal preparation down to a science: run down during a commercial break during her afternoon shows, be back before the show resumed, and have dinner on the table by the next commercial break. Occasionally we would get a reprieve when my father would roll out the barbecue. Hamburgers, hot dogs, and an occasional steak were a welcome change.

Fridays were an adventure. Being Roman Catholics, meat was not an option that day, but it was Charlie the Tuna to the rescue. This was our gourmet meal for the week. Once she opened the can and threw in a bit of mayo, she placed this on a leaf of lettuce on my plate. Until college, I thought that was the use for lettuce, to rest under a scoop of tuna. We, of course, did not eat the lettuce, which I thought was just mutant parsley. We never had a salad, and I remember, at age sixteen, being served a salad at a friend's house. As they all dug in, I stared at them in complete disbelief. They were eating leaves! I thought only rabbits and deer did that. I ate everything else on my plate, working around the pile of leaves, until my friend's mother finally said, "Don't you like salad?" So that's what they call it. Wanting to be a proper and appreciative guest, I drowned it in salad dressing and easily consumed it.

But these Friday tuna meals became a staple. They appeared Friday after Friday. My sister also noticed the pattern and began tallying how many consecutive Fridays that tuna showed up in front of us. Fifty-four Fridays in a row! The routine was broken one Friday night when Mom and Dad left for a party before dinner. We hid the cans of tuna from the babysitter and got peanut butter and jelly sandwiches. Never has a PB&J sandwich tasted so good. We then informed the sitter that we always had ice cream for dessert every night, and we quickly dove into my mother's sacred stash of frozen dairy desserts. No Jell-O that night. She did try to make pudding once, but it somehow ended up as one big indigestible lump. I remember thinking that it might be alive as it began to pulse. My brother Bill ate it and even went back for seconds, but then he once ate mothballs.

Mom remembered everyone's birthday. She never once forgot the birthdays of anyone in her large family: every child, sibling, nephew, niece, cousin, or second cousin twice removed. It was impressive. We got a birthday cake for every birthday after my mother discovered a wonderful bakery in Hampden. They also made great rolls and pies, and these started appearing with some frequency. God bless Silber's Bakery. But when Christmas came rolling around, the cookie cupboard was always bare except for what friends and relatives sent us. When I was ten and my sister nine, we knew we needed to address the problem. A trip down the hill to see our grandmother was what the doctor ordered; she had been our savior many times before. Throughout a couple of afternoons, she taught us both how to bake. No Christmas should ever pass without the odor of Toll House cookies baking in the kitchen.

Gussie and I returned home from our baking lesson, sending my mother off to the store with a list of ingredients. She happily obliged, and soon the kitchen was ready for a day of fun and games. We mixed enough dough to feed the entire U.S. Army, and soon the oven was ready to turn this dough into melt-in-your-mouth treasures. That is, until Gussie, Bill, and I discovered that the raw dough tasted great also. We started eating as much dough as went into the cookies. And, of course, we had to take several samples from each batch we cooked. One also has to taste them at varying stages of cooling. We baked away from lunch until dinner. Never had our kitchen seen such activity. Strangely when dinner time arrived, we were not hungry. Even stranger, after six hours of baking, we managed to fill up only one cookie tin. Not surprisingly, we were both far too sick to go to school the next day. When the next weekend came, the chocolate chip cookie factory went into high gear again, with better intestinal results.

No birthday passed without a cake after that, as my sister and I could roll one out of the oven. My mother sadly passed away several years ago, and she was able to move on with a spotless record—no cookie or cake ever baked. If the reader ever makes it to heaven and Mom is staffing the kitchen up there, you might want to head down below. At least things will get cooked down there.

But breakfast was Mom's forte. Once again, to her credit, she got up every school morning to cook us breakfast. No child of hers would hit the road without food on board. Unlike many today, she knew the value of a good breakfast; she just had trouble with the "good" part. Again, variation was not the order of the day: orange juice, cereal, and fried eggs. It was by accident years later that I discovered one could do something different with an egg other than frying it: scrambled eggs. Cereal during the summer was the high point in that she gave in to the sugary cereal appetite of her kids and bought us the latest brand touted during Saturday morning cartoons. The best part of the cereal was that some prize was always included somewhere in the box. It was against the rules to fish around in the box, so one had to wait until it rolled out in your bowl. One might have to consume three or four heaping bowls of cereal before the secret decoder ring rolled out. Who was the sick Kelloggs executive who decided the toy needed to be at the bottom of the box? And shaking the box only drove the toy deeper.

But winter was when breakfast moved front and center in the Culinary House of Horrors. This was when Mom did things to oatmeal that should have been illegal. I don't know what real oatmeal is supposed to taste like. People consume it, so it must be good. The only way to envision Mom's version of the breakfast stable is to imagine a mixture of wallpaper paste and golf balls. Mom might have used golf balls since, later, we lived a block away from a golf course. The oatmeal lumps were so hard I would bet they were indigestible. There was no way to chew them; they had to be swallowed whole. An adult could push one down, but they weren't going down a child's gullet. Somehow, Dixie the Beagle could get them down, and she became my constant breakfast companion. The pasty texture of the oatmeal was a different matter. In attempting to swallow this, it would become lodged in your throat, seeming to harden with time. Repeated attempts to get it to the esophagus made one look like they were gagging, and in fact, that's what was happening. Only copious amounts of orange juice, our breakfast Drano, could break the clog, sending it on its merry way. We once patched a hole in the closet floor with it, and, who knows, it will outlast the wood. My father got coffee instead of oatmeal; it was, I guess, a form of torture reserved only for children.

Or maybe it was an evolutionary test; anyone who could survive it must have the constitution to live a long and happy life. And I have!

When I was eight, my youngest sister Kim was born, and Mom was in the hospital for five days, a real contrast to today's pop it out and send them home approach. While we missed Mom, we rejoiced at the cook taking some time off until we met the replacement cook, Dad. While he could barbecue, he was not comfortable in the kitchen. He had learned to cook one menu item in the military service. He called this a "Birmingham egg." Don't bother googling it; it apparently never caught on. He would cut a hole in a slice of bread, put it in a pan, and drop an egg in the hole. It was not bad, but this was the *only* thing he could cook. And for five days, we ate them for breakfast and dinner; school lunches were our only salvation.

In the early 1960s, Mom discovered something which would change our lives forever—the TV dinner. Dinners took on a fresh look from this point on. These started as a quick meal when a babysitter came in, but she soon discovered they worked simply fine for a regular dinner. These and chicken pot pies became a staple at our house. From freezer to oven to table with almost no effort—Mom thought she had died and gone to heaven. The sad thing is that these were a big hit, a marked improvement over the usual staple. Someone should have bought Swanson stock back in 1960s because our family must have pushed that stock into outer space.

When my wife-to-be Jackie and I met in college, I told her some of the legendary tales of my mother's cooking. She laughed but thought I had exaggerated a wee bit. And when she visited our home for the first time, Mom did spend a whole hour in the kitchen preparing Jackie's inaugural meal. I remember the dinner vividly. As it was a warm summer evening, we ate on the side porch. As Mom brought out the first round of plates, I eagerly looked to see what would appear, hoping she had learned to cook while I was at college. She lowered the first plate, and there it was: tuna fish on a leaf of lettuce, canned peas, and instant mashed potatoes. Then the fun began. I watched Jackie take her fork to pick up the mashed potatoes. Before the fork was halfway to her mouth, all the potatoes had run through the tines and fallen back to her plate. Trying to make an excellent first impression, she tried again but to no avail. My father watched and tried hard to stifle a laugh. Jackie changed her strategy, next trying to rush the fork to her mouth before the runny potatoes could fall back to her plate. No luck! She tried again, even faster this time, but the potatoes still ran back onto the plate. I couldn't hold back the laughter anymore. When asked why I was laughing, I replied, "I heard a funny story today, Mom."

Jackie finally discovered that if she tilted the fork back with the tines up, she could get small bits of potatoes at a time. And to her credit, she kept her cool, telling Mom at the end of the meal how delicious it had been. This was the first of many meals Jackie ate in the Culinary House of Horrors.

After Jackie and I married, Mom, to her credit, would always host a birthday party for each of us. Even if the culinary part of her brain was dysfunctional, her heart was always in the right place. We joined them for many years, and the menu never varied: fried chicken from English's Chicken in town, potato chips, and Jell-O. The chicken came out on a platter after being warmed in the oven, but all knew where it came from. The chips came out in a nice bowl; they must taste better that way. But her Jell-O was an upgrade over what we got as kids. It had cherries in it and cottage cheese on top. This was Mom's upgraded pièce de résistance. Tragically, English's Chicken went out of business, and Mom, obviously in the initial stages of dementia, decided to try to bake a chicken on one fateful birthday. If we had only known what was in store, we all would have made alternative plans.

The family was shocked as the platter came out, not with the usual fried chicken, but one that was baked. It passed the initial visual inspection, and we were all both surprised and delighted … that was until we bit into it. As my teeth sank into it, I hit a bone where there shouldn't have been. Dissecting it, I soon realized the center was still frozen. The others had already noticed the meat was still red. No one wanted to hurt my mother's feelings, but we had to get the bird back in the oven tactfully. We finally suggested it might help to "heat it a bit." That was the last meal my mother ever cooked. She and Dad moved into a retirement home soon after, and he wisely chose the comprehensive meal plan. The world would now be spared.

It's hard to talk about her past cooking now that she's moved on. Everyone has an Achilles' heel, and I'm not known for my culinary expertise. There's a tendency not to speak ill of the dead, but I choose to remember people as they were. We'll often deify someone who has passed, but this is when they cease to be a real person. And no one was more real than my mother. She was kind and the most unselfish person I have ever known, always putting others' needs before hers. There was no better mother—if only she had just stayed out of the kitchen.

Armageddon in Baltimore: September 20, 1958

Ours was a peaceful city neighborhood: the sounds of children playing, barking dogs, the distant sounds of cars. Although in the heart of the city, our narrow, tree-lined neighborhood was a calm oasis in an otherwise busy and noisy world. However, the peace and tranquility were rudely interrupted one cool September afternoon by an event that undoubtedly caused property values to tumble and which likely precipitated our family's move soon after. September 20, 1958, was a day that will live in infamy—well, for our family, it certainly was.

Saturday began peacefully, not that any house with four young children could be quiet. While the anticipation of the upcoming party was evident throughout the Radcliffe house, no one could have foretold the events which would play out before the sun set. That morning, all appeared normal. Neighborhood children played outside, chased outside by parents needing some moments of peace, and dogs barked as they chased a rare vehicle up our narrow street. Our house buzzed with excitement as all was in place for the Big Event, or so we thought. It was my brother Bill's fifth birthday, and nothing would be quite the same again.

We will never know what possessed my parents to invite twenty little boys to a party in our home. Bill's birthday was the next day, but Saturday was chosen as the day for the party. God forbid someone has a party on the same afternoon as a Baltimore Colts football game. Unlike today when people pay good money to hire an outfit to entertain the little ones while the parents become only spectators, this was a time when parents did all the work. There was no Chuck E. Cheese or McDonald's Playland at that time, and the job of party planner did not exist. It fell on the parents' shoulders to completely orchestrate the event. My parents deserve much credit for hosting the event; however, they made one fatal error, which they lived to regret. For a party three hours in length, they planned absolutely no activities beyond eating ice cream and cake. The assembled energizer bunnies had no trouble filling up the three hours, much to my parents' horror. When the dust settled at four in the afternoon, and quiet was restored to Baltimore, the aftermath of a tornado would have been less impressive. We moved two months later, unable to ever salvage what was once a delightful home.

Most families on that narrow street had young children, enough young ones to almost warrant our own school. Throw in two or three cousins, and it was not difficult to fill our house with young boys. My sister, age seven, and I, just nine, were to be present to assist and watch our little sister Kim, fifteen months old. My father was not worried at all, even taking the time that morning to read the paper and do some garden work in our minute yard. My mother, who didn't bake, had purchased a large cake and loaded up with a large quantity of her favorite ice-cold milk derivative, making sure she sampled it numerous times before the guests arrived. The table was set, and all was ready for what promised to be a wonderful celebration. Bill, typically boisterous and delightfully hyperactive, drooled at the thought of all the presents he would receive.

The first guests arrived just before one o'clock, each bearing a gift. As the presents started to pile in the living room, Bill, boiling over with excitement, kept asking to begin opening the gifts. When the last boy and gift arrived, the mountain of gifts rose halfway to the ceiling. My father was there, but only two other moms were there to assist. This was when taking a child to a birthday party was a mom's job. Fathers were busy that day doing "man's work," such as drinking beer or watching a college football game. These poor moms had no idea early that afternoon what lay in store for them.

My father gave the word, and Bill quickly charged into the task of opening all the presents, with his sister Gussie orchestrating the unwrapping. The kids squealed with glee as each gift was unmasked. Bill would take a glance at the gift before diving into the next. The gifts were nice by today's standards with thankfully no plastic toys: metal trucks and cars, a few toy pistols, a bow with rubber-tipped arrows, games, and sports equipment. As the last present was opened, the boys lost the last of their restraint and dove in, each grabbing one of the presents to play with. Excitement quickly turned to chaos, and the moms, in a moment of panic, promptly ushered the five-year-old crowd into the dining room for cake and ice cream. Cake trumps toys any day. The only problem was that it was only one fifteen; the moms were playing their ace card early in what was to be a long afternoon. Mom carried in the cake, and her crew dished out the ice cream. Mom had purchased two cakes from the local bakery, and ice cream flowed. She had gone all out, and there were party hats and favors. But this was where she made another fatal error. Sitting beside each child's place was a paddle ball, a popular toy in the 1950s consisting of a ball attached to a paddle by a long rubber band. One could whack the ball with the paddle, and after flying out into the room, the ball would be pulled back by the band. This might be an excellent point to note that there were floor-to-ceiling glass doors and windows between our living room and hallway. Mom and the other parents should have realized what would happen later when these toys were unleashed on the house. However, all was under control as the kids squealed with glee, stuffing ice cream and cake down their throats. Amazingly, most of the ice cream and cake made it into their mouths.

There were napkins, but what five-year-old uses a napkin when there are tablecloths, clothes, and walls readily available?

Mom was pleased that all was going so well, but that was before she looked at her watch. "Oh no, it's just one thirty!!! What do we do now?" That question was answered as the kids charged back into the living room to play with the presents. Mistake number four—no one thought to clean the kids up as forty sticky and crumby hands rushed out into our house, some still carrying large chunks of cake. We never did figure out how a scoop of ice cream ended up in a vase on the mantlepiece, and the chocolate handprint motif on all the walls was impressive.

The sequence of events gets confusing at this point. Several activities were going on simultaneously. The cowboys and Indians were battling it out on the second floor, and a spontaneous tackle football game was taking place in the living room. Gussie was leading a comeback by the vastly outnumbered Indians as doors continuously slammed. The screams of the cowboys crescendoed as they retreated down the steps and through the football game in the living room. The fact that no one had picked up any wrapping paper from the earlier unveiling added to the growing chaos. Without missing a beat, a couple of the Indians joined the football game, and some of the players reinforced the cowboys, causing the tide to turn. The conflict now moved back up the stairs, and the Indians retreated to my parents' bedroom. Stories conflicted about how my parents' newly purchased television ended up on the floor, never to work again, but the crash sent the adults racing up the steps. One of the stories had Gussie bouncing up and down on the bed, trying to inspire the remaining Indians until one errant bounce sent her flying into the set. Who knows! Who cares? Gussie was unphased and led the Indians on a new offensive.

As parents tried cleaning up the mess upstairs, one of the kids discovered the paddle party favors. Within minutes, every kid was paddling away with balls flying in every possible direction. Two or three were crying as these kids got a much-too-close look at the flying projectiles. At one point, one of the cowboys made the discovery of the day—these paddle balls made great weapons. One could hit the ball with a paddle, watch it fly off and hit someone, and then return quickly to your paddle. At this point, the football game ended, and the previous cowboy and Indian war went into hyperdrive. Because there were twenty balls continuously in flight around the room, it is remarkable that only a picture frame, a vase, and one window were broken. Gussie, realizing that the Indians were in trouble, quickly led their retreat down into the basement.

My job was to assist with the activities, although no one had ever explained what the activities were supposed to be. I became a spectator, and the more chaotic things became, the more I enjoyed the show. I knew the basement was off limits to us when our friends were here, but I was having too much fun to stop this. It was an unfinished basement with two rooms, a laundry room, and a dark room with a dirt floor with old coal residue. Before I could go down to see what was happening, and I was in no hurry since there was leftover candy on the table, I heard the Indians mounting another charge up the steps. They emerged with a mighty battle cry wearing sheets and towels and dirtier than when they had retreated down the steps. The battle reached its climax as the cowboys tried to withstand the new attack, complete with guns, a bow and arrow captured from the Indians, and an array of paddle ball weapons. As the Indians continued to gain ground, the cowboys retreated into the dining room, which the parents had failed to finish cleaning once the TV set hit the floor. The cowboys hid under the table while the Indians raced around the table, screaming and occasionally stopping for another handful of cake. The cowboys suddenly lost interest in the battle because they had carried the bowl of remaining chocolates under the table. That's when another crash sent the parents running for the dining room. Somehow the midget warriors had moved a leg supporting a table wing, sending cake, dishes, glasses, and who knows what else crashing to the floor. My mother had since retreated to a couch, dissolving in tears, and my father was back outside gardening ... clearly in complete denial.

And so, the fun continued. My memory gets fuzzy at this point. I do remember a tricycle being thrown down the steps at one point, clothes raining down outside the living room window as the contents of my brother's bureau somehow made it outside his window, and a stream of milk flowing into the dining room from a broken milk bottle in the kitchen. The parents sat in the living room dumbfounded, staring at the clock, which my mother repeatedly checked, thinking it had stopped.

Somehow four o'clock finally arrived that day, and the house grew quieter, one kid at a time. When the last child left, my parents collapsed into chairs in our living room for a significantly longer-than-normal cocktail hour. Gussie, Bill, Kim, and I retreated upstairs under strict parental orders.

It was only later that day that we realized the full extent of the damage:

- Muddy/sooty footprints, too numerous to count, leading from the basement door and extending into every room in the house.
- Chocolate ice cream handprints up and down the staircase and coating every piece of living room furniture
- Clothes and laundry littered every room of the house and outdoors
- Chocolate stomped into every carpet in the house
- Wrapping paper residue throughout the house
- One toilet stopped up with wrapping paper still floating in the bowl; my father also later retrieved two toy soldiers which were hiding in the drainpipe leading from the toilet

- Enough breakage to fill up the garbage for several weeks
- A now non-operational television set—this was when a set cost nearly as much as a car!
- And not one of the twenty presents survived intact— how does one break a metal truck?

We moved to a larger house less than two months later. This might have been a coincidence, but I believe the party motivated the decision. Quite possibly, we were evicted from the neighborhood, or my parents decided that moving was easier than repairing all the damage. I went by the house many times after we moved, and it remained standing. I'll never forget that wonderful day when chaos reigned supreme.

One of the terrible stereotypes of the 1950s dealt with cowboys and Native Americans, referred to as "Indians" at that time. Countless TV programs and movies portrayed these two groups as constantly at war, with the cowboys usually portrayed as the good guys. Thankfully, we have moved past this period with a more accurate portrayal of these groups. Children's play often reflects the battle between good and evil forces, and, sadly, children raised in the 1950s were subjected to this stereotype, with so many of our games reflecting these images. However, with Gussie leading the Indian brigade, the cowboys were completely outmatched this time.

When my tenth birthday came up for discussion, it was my turn to have a party, and I had big plans. My parents listened to my request and then said, "Let's have your party at Jimmy Wu's restaurant. You can invite two friends." No one in our family ever had a large birthday party again.

THE CHRISTMAS THAT
ALMOST WASN'T

The Christmas of 1959 was one for the ages, but then all our Christmases were. The holiday was steeped in tradition and ritual, which screamed "family, love, and caring" in our household. My parents orchestrated a Christmas to top them all. While the gifts were never excessive, the elaborate ritual we all followed made it as joyous an occasion as any child could experience. Christmas disasters were not foreign to our family. The one Christmas Day that all of us vomited the whole day had to have been particularly joyous for my mother, almost as much fun as the one where we awoke to no water and a foot of water in the basement.

This was our second year in a new house, and all was ready for another wild and wooly Radcliffe family Christmas. At age ten, I graduated to being Santa's assistant, and as the oldest sibling, I enjoyed this new position of power. Santa's role on Christmas Eve was not insignificant as everything would happen after the children went to bed, from decorating the tree, mantle, and windows to assembling the many presents. My father had pulled off this gargantuan task alone for years while my mother searched for hours for those two or three presents she had hidden in a place she would be sure to find. They would both get to bed just as we were getting ready to head downstairs in the morning. I had always wondered why my parents took a nap on Christmas afternoon until I began to assist. My sister,

Gussie, had been filled in on the true nature of Santa this year, and it was my job to explain the details to her. She was in complete denial, even after all my explanations, and chose to go to bed early with my brother and younger sister. God forbid she should break tradition. After waiting an hour or so for the two of them to fall asleep, the massive transformation began.

My father was meticulously organized, undoubtedly a product of his military experience as an aircraft maintenance officer during World War II. The presents were stored in a cedar closet on the third floor of the house; all had been previously wrapped and labeled by my mother. The tree trimmings were in well-organized and labeled boxes. When my siblings were asleep, it would be my job to carry the boxes from the third floor down to the first, moving carefully and quietly past the bedrooms of my sleeping siblings. My father was pumping out Christmas Carols downstairs, and this would provide any necessary background to drown out my travels up and down the steps. Now that Santa had an assistant, my mother was turning in early, her job of wrapping presents long ago completed, and the two misplaced presents were finally found. Additionally, she found a third present, lost from a previous Christmas.

At 8:45 PM, I headed up for the first load of presents. The key was usually kept on a narrow ledge above the door, but it disappeared a few weeks before Christmas each year in case certain juvenile intrepid explorers decided to use the cedar closet as a hiding place or base of covert operations during one of our imaginative training exercises. Dad had said the key was on his bureau, but a brief search revealed no key. After he could not locate it, he informed me there was no cause for concern as he had spares made of every key. He handed me a box and told me to go through it until I could find the right key. I lugged the box to the third floor and opened the lid, seeing several hundred keys. Dad was downstairs wiring the tree to the wall so that there was no way it could topple, and I began the slow process of trying every one of the keys. Not one of them worked.

After sharing this critical update with Dad, he, still unconcerned, joined me on the third floor and proceeded to go through every key individually. As the pile of untried keys dwindled, his expression changed, and his jovial banter quickly evolved into silence. Once the magnitude of the evolving situation became apparent, his smile evaporated. And this was no ordinary door. It was a rock-solid door that opened from the inside, and there would be no popping off door jamb molding and jimmying the lock. Mom was oblivious to this as she had turned in to watch her nightly television show, and Dad went down to the living room to ponder the situation.

He quickly decided that there would be no way to get a locksmith late on Christmas Eve, and breaking down the door would either be impossible or so disruptive as to awaken the whole house (and probably the neighborhood). Logic prevailed, and he soon realized that with two keys somewhere in the house, we could undoubtedly find one of them. Thus commenced the search of a lifetime: every room, every drawer, every one of his 2,017 meticulously organized and labeled storage boxes. We searched and searched and searched. Amazingly, although worried, he never lost his cool or muttered any unmentionable words, which he had undoubtedly learned and perfected years earlier in the military. When one's life is in danger in a wartime situation, the last thing one needs to worry about is the quality of one's vocabulary.

At about 10:30, Mom emerged from her cave, sensing something was wrong. She didn't curse, but then she never did. She said nothing, as no words could have gotten past the sobbing which soon erupted. Finally, she was able to make one request of my father, "George, do something!" That wonderful advice almost brought forth the heretofore unuttered vocabulary. Dad kept his cool, simply telling Mom to go back to bed. That wasn't going to happen to the Crown Princess of Worrying. She joined the search, sobbing every step of the way. It was approaching 11 PM, and the family emergency level was now elevated to DEFCON 1. All began to realize that Christmas might not happen this year, delayed until we could eventually locate a locksmith. We discussed how we would explain that Santa was coming a couple of days late, especially since he would visit the houses on either side of us. The scenarios flew right and left. Maybe Dad forgot to put out the fire in the fireplace, which he never did anyway, a fact that had puzzled me years earlier. We could leave a note from Santa saying he left something at the North Pole and would bring everything on a second trip. None of the stories would work, and we soon realized it was time for an act of desperation.

Out came the tools. We already knew there would be no way to cut through the door. Today's doors are often so flimsy one could cut through them with a utility knife, but this door was built to last. There was going to be no getting through it. There had to be a way to get through the lock or jimmy it somehow, but how would we do this without walking three sleeping children on the floor below? It might be hard explaining to them that Santa needed a sledgehammer to accomplish his mission. And a quick look at the door construction made it clear that a sledgehammer would have been useless anyway. After we tried removing molding and manipulating the lock, it was clear that this door and lock were built to last and possibly even survive a nuclear blast. Dad still kept his cool.

Retreating to the first floor, a serious meeting ensued. One of the perks of being an older sibling on Christmas Eve is eating Santa's cookies. These had been devoured long ago, and I was now deep into the mother lode, supposedly hidden but found earlier in the day by this intrepid detective. I could hear the argument from the other room.

"George, you just have to get into that closet."

"I've tried everything."

"Then do something else."

"What, Gussie? I've done everything."

"But you have to get in there. Call a locksmith."

"At 11 PM on Christmas Eve. Have you lost your mind!"

"But at least you can try." One of Mom's endearing and sometimes frustrating qualities was her persistence. To her, nothing was impossible, and "quit" was not in her vocabulary.

The argument stopped here. Out came the phone book, and we soon learned there were twelve listed locksmiths in Baltimore. Mom quickly commanded, "Start calling." Dad informed her that every one of these numbers was a store, and no one would be in their store at that hour, especially on Christmas Eve. Mom's response was a simple order, "Call anyway."

He began dialing the numbers one by one getting the expected no answer. This was long before answering machines, and the phone would just ring and ring. He finally got to the last of the twelve numbers, and we waited desperately as the phone rang continuously. No answer. Dejected, Dad put down the phone. He was now wholly resigned to a Christmas nightmare.

Ever optimistic, Mom quickly chimed in, "Well, try them all again."

"Gussie, it's 11:30, and no one is at their store."

"George, you can't give up. Keep calling."

"But...."

"CALL!"

Dad wore the pants in the family but never refused Mom's requests. Tonight, she was a determined drill sergeant. Obediently, he began calling each number again. This was a futile activity, but Mom was going to have him dial numbers until someone answered. He made it through the entire list again with no answer. Mom quickly prompted him, "Try again."

The continuous dialing followed by pauses was all I could hear from the kitchen. I was prepared for the disappointment of the next day, but I worried about how my brother and sisters would react.

That wasn't going to be a pretty sight. I imagined the tantrum Gussie would throw when I suddenly heard Dad talking. "Hello, this is George Radcliffe. I'm so sorry to bother you, but …." I raced into the living room to hear him pleading with the voice on the other end of the phone. He pulled out all the stops: "Christmas would be ruined," and "children's hopes would be dashed." I soon heard him giving out our address, and the impossible seemed about to happen.

Dad explained that the gentleman had said he could come, but it would be an hour before he could get there, as he had to get dressed and was located on the other side of the city. And, of course, there was still no guarantee that he could get the door open. That was a long hour. Dickens' "A Christmas Carol" was on TV, and I was soon lost in that. It was Christmas Day already, and Mom and Dad were far too nervous to watch TV. They talked and worried. I continued my assault on the Christmas cookies, which I felt entitled to since Gussie and I had baked most of them anyway.

I heard the doorbell ring at about 1 AM, and I raced down the steps to join the activity. A short, simply dressed, elderly gentleman, carrying one of the most enormous work boxes I had ever seen, stood at the door. Dad led him up the stairs, repeatedly apologizing for getting him out at this hour. The man explained that he lived above his shop and that when he heard the phone ring for the third time, he figured he had better answer it. He looked at the lock and quickly turned around. "I'm not sure I have a key for this lock. It's a most unusual lock, the first one I've ever seen installed in a house." Our hearts sank, but he began methodically going through his incredible array of keys and gadgets. Most of his keys would not fit into the hole and those that did failed to turn. Then suddenly, one turned in the lock, and the door was open before we realized what was happening. Christmas was saved. And there, on a suitcase right inside the door, sat the key. Neither of my parents ever admitted to leaving it there.

The thanks and praises flew at the gentleman like arrows, but he only smiled slightly as we walked back down to the first floor. He gave my father a bill for five dollars, his usual fee with no overtime or special charge added. My father gave him a twenty-dollar bill, and my mother gave him a large box of candy. I don't remember the name of this Christmas Day saint who saved a Christmas for our family. He's one of the many nameless people selflessly doing their job. He had sacrificed several precious hours on a special night when he easily could not have answered that phone or responded with, "I'll see you on the twenty-sixth." I thought of him several times the next day. We get so wrapped up in our own lives that we soon forget that the entire world does not revolve around us, but we only had a Christmas that day because of him. His name was quickly forgotten, but his selfless actions never were.

Mom and Dad quickly fixed themselves a drink, beaming from ear to ear. It was almost 2 AM, no Christmas setup had been done, and my siblings would be at their door in less than four hours, but sleep was not the thing on their minds. Dad and I got the tree decorated by 3 AM and were admiring it when we heard my mother scream. We raced into the kitchen to see Nickie, the family beagle, madly devouring the garbage she now had strewn over the kitchen floor. The commotion had finally awoken her, and ignored, she soon found an irresistible treat. Life was officially back to normal now. I may have slept briefly that night, but I'm sure my parents didn't. And when Gussie and Bill piled into their room at 5:45 AM, they were not sent back to bed. Rising quickly, my father said, as he always did, "I wonder if Santa came last night." He certainly did that night in the form of a little old man lugging the world's most extensive collection of keys.

The Real Spirit of Christmas

*On one special Christmas, my Uncle Teddy Hartman shared a story
with me that forever defines the true spirit of Christmas.
Not a Christmas goes by without my trying to put
myself in his place in the Christmas of 1944.*

On Christmas Day, 1944, eighteen-year-old Teddy stood silently
in formation in Stalag Luft IV, a POW camp in what is now
northwestern Poland. As punishment for their mischievous attempts
to disrupt life at the camp for the Germans, he and the other prisoners of war were prohibited from celebrating Christmas. They were
not allowed to decorate a tree or mention the holiday in any way.
Homesickness pervaded the camp on even an ordinary day, but the
loneliness ran deep that day. Memories flowed of holidays past with
families, but the only carol that day was the howling of the chilly
winter winds outside. As he stood motionless in formation in the
barracks, he dreamed of a Christmas in a warm house surrounded
by family and gifts. A fantastic set of circumstances had landed him
in a POW camp, and he was far removed from the patriotic youth
who had enlisted to serve his country. Even singing a few carols
would have gotten him through the day, but he only heard silence as
the Americans stood under the watchful eye of the armed German
guards. But something unusual and memorable was about to occur.

Teddy had enlisted at the age of seventeen and was stationed with
the 836th Bombardment Squadron in England. He was a tail gunner

on a B-17, and on November 9, 1944, his plane was shot down over Germany after a bombing run. Several of the crew died, and he barely escaped death on several occasions. After a brief period in a concentration camp, he was transported to Stalag Luft IV, an internment camp for enlistees. With his infectious wit, he and the others in the camp had worked overtime, disrupting life in the camp: performing tasks at the slowest rate possible, spilling everything, tormenting the guards, and pretending to be hard of hearing when commands were issued. However, having every vestige of Christmas taken away sucked the energy from any remaining morale.

The Americans had asked to sing Christmas carols to salvage even the slightest hint of Christmas, but even that request had been denied. This seemed like such an innocent request on a holiday when so many of the prisoners had to be feeling so much emotion. Christmas has always been a time to reflect on family and one's life, and to be a prisoner in a distant land had to accentuate every emotion significantly. The troops accepted the decree but had to stand in formation for much of the day. Standing in silence allowed the memories to flow unabated, and all the prisoners knew what the others were thinking and feeling. Teddy remembered many of the thoughts that ran through his head during those hours: What was his family doing? Would this be the last Christmas he would ever have? Did they know how much he missed them? While he was lucky to be alive, loneliness dominated his thoughts.

Suddenly, he heard the faintest of sounds and strained to detect what it was. One of the prisoners had begun to hum *Silent Night* ever so quietly. Ironically, this was a German carol (*Stille Nacht, Heilige Nacht*), although composed by Austrian Franz Gruber with lyrics written by Joseph Mohr. Before long, a second prisoner joined in, the humming still barely perceptible. Then a third and a fourth commenced humming until the whole troop was humming in unison. Teddy waited for the German guards to intervene, but this never happened. The humming crescendoed, and surprisingly none of the Germans reacted. He knew they weren't singing the carol, but the guards would undoubtedly want to quelch this. Even though he was supposed to be only looking straight ahead, Teddy dared a glance to the side, and to his surprise, he noticed tears running down the closest guard's face. The humming continued for quite a while, and soon there was no dry eye in the barracks. Never was there a simpler yet more profound celebration of the holiday. All were carried away by emotion and united. For one brief moment, the war was miles away, and Christmas was likely the only thing that could have bridged the gap between captors and prisoners.

Hansel and Gretel, Part 2

(Ode to Margaret Hamilton)

The three of us sat in a dimly lit room in a strange house, knowing death was imminent. I thought of my family that I would never see again and of all my life plans that would never come to fruition. How did I get talked into the predicament I now found myself in: sitting there with no one knowing my whereabouts? We should have run, but fear paralyzed us. The only remaining question was how I would die. I saw the headline: "The bodies of three Baltimore youths were found today, the victims of a bizarre and horrific ritual." That particular Halloween evening, Jack, Frank, and I, driven by greed, had ventured out of our familiar Baltimore neighborhood; an overflowing bag of candy was not enough for each of us. We had broken the two cardinal Halloween rules. My mother's instructions were to stay in the neighborhood, but a friend had easily talked me into leaving and heading into an area where we knew no one. Rule two was common sense to all: never knock on a door where the outdoor light was not turned on. But this house was large and intriguing, and we had struck gold, or should I say chocolate, on this street. And we wanted more! We now sat awaiting our fate.

Halloween is at the core of many childhood memories with its trick-or-treating, costumes, and all-important candy. Sadly, as with most holidays in American culture, it has become so over-commercialized in recent years, with approximately six billion dollars being spent on it each year in the U.S. Happily, it has become a much safer day than in years past, a fact motivated by the news today where we obsess over every little incident which does occur. We still use the term "trick or treat," but the emphasis today is far more on the "treat" than the "trick."

In my parents' childhood, the "trick or treat" placed far more emphasis on trickery. Practical jokes abounded: ringing doorbells and running, draping a neighbor's trees with toilet paper, and jumping out and scaring people. A treat from the individual would spare one the trick. Apples, bread, and cakes made up the bulk of the goodies. By my childhood, the candy industry was starting to sink its teeth into the tradition, and now one-quarter of the candy sold in the United States annually is purchased for this one day. I ate a substantial portion of that tonnage on that final day in October. In my trick-or-treating days, the trickery was on the decline but had become a little more malicious with an occasional fire, throwing eggs, or roughing up a younger child for their candy. After I outgrew the holiday, I, with nothing better to do, would usually accompany my younger siblings to help protect them and their candy from neighborhood teens. I had one acquaintance who collected dog manure in small brown paper bags and lit it on fire on a neighbor's doorstep. The poor soul would stomp on the fire, and ... you can guess the rest. I would never have stooped this low, but as a teen, I always traveled with a can of shaving cream to defend myself or, more likely, decorate a friend. One Halloween, a friend and I pummeled one kid with eggs and shaving cream after hearing that he had jumped my little brother and stolen all his candy. Bill ended up with not only his candy but considerably more that year. We had one older woman who was pleasant to no one, and we would fill her mailbox with shaving cream, our revenge for not being allowed in her yard to retrieve our errant baseballs. Others did far worse to her, but I always felt a little sorry for the miserable and friendless soul. However, she did deserve an annual shaving cream cleansing.

But the candy was what the day was about, and we would travel everywhere, amassing as large a haul of candy as possible, even returning home on occasion to retrieve a second bag. When I was young, my candy was passed to my parents and allocated to me over several days, but I soon learned to hide a stash of the good stuff in my room. I would always convince myself that I could stretch out the supply for days, but my poor digestive system invariably suffered a massive onslaught that night and the next day. It is utterly amazing that our septic system survived the deluge. My Grandmother Radcliffe, whose life's pursuit had become spoiling her grandchildren, won the prize as she gave us each a one-pound candy bar each year. Yes, that's one pound, sixteen glorious ounces of irresistible chocolate. My mother tried to get her to stop this, but no one ever told my grandmother what to do … ever!

People were less worried about safety when I was young, and we could roam the streets, collecting as much candy as we could carry. We lived in a neighborhood with row houses, and there was a cornucopia of candy to be had. We would even venture onto adjoining streets where we knew no one. If they left their light on, we would be knocking on that door. I remember feeling guilty about taking candy from a stranger, but candy trumped any guilt. Most were glad to see us, and some even asked who we were. This particular year, greed had driven my two friends and I far from our neighborhood; working three or four complete blocks, we had just come to the last house. There was no outdoor light on, but we could see a couple of lights inside the house. Any fear of knocking on the doors of strange homes was long gone, and we could barely carry our haul up the long flight of steps. We knocked, and an older man answered. "What do you want?" he asked. This seemed a strange question to ask a group of kids dressed as superman, monsters, and ghosts. "Trick or treat" was the obvious response, and he stood expressionless, staring at us a while before finally saying, "Come inside." That wasn't one of the possible responses we had anticipated, but being the fools that we were, we entered. "Sit in the living room, and we'll be right with you." Still no hint of a smile!

The room was lit only by several candles, and we gazed around the room while we waited. The room smelled dusty as the shelves were stocked full of books. There were small ornate statues throughout the room, and I remember that the array of prisms hanging from the candleholders sent little sparks of light across the room. As if the room were not eerie enough, some mysterious classical organ music came from the next room. (See Bach's Toccata and Fugue in D Minor.) We waited for an eternity and were finally starting to get nervous. We glanced at each other, and I'm sure all were waiting for one of us to make a move to leave.

Why were we waiting since these people were not in the usual Halloween mode? One of my friends said, "Maybe they're going to murder us all?" That did it, but none of us dared to make the first move. Suddenly a much older woman, clearly but subtly dressed as a witch, came through the curtain. Her face was rugged, tanned, and wrinkled, and her long grey hair flowed past her shoulders; no make-up was needed here. The music grew louder. "What's wrong, children? Have you never seen a real witch before?" I had been out long enough to need to use a bathroom, and that comment almost sent my urine toward a faster-than-planned exit. The older man was now walking in with a large pot, with steam rising from it. The "witch" added, "This is my witches brew, and I know you all will have some." Were we to end up as part of the soup served to the next band of children? This was Hansel and Gretel come to fruition! Then I remembered that I had never seen any kids going to this door while working both sides of that street that evening. We were in real trouble. I would have run for the door, but the older gentleman was now standing in front of it. The woman started singing some incomprehensible chant over the pot, and this was when two other witches entered the room, all muttering the same chant. Was this the "grace" before we became part of the meal?

Raised on *The Wizard of Oz*, we all knew how evil witches were. No one believed that Glinda the Good Witch was a witch because Margaret Hamilton, as the Wicked Witch of the West, defined witches for years. Never was a Best Supporting Actress Academy Award more deserving as she gave more children of our generation nightmares than any other cinematic character. While none of the three witches in front of us that evening could rival Margaret, our imaginations made up the difference. We would be incinerated, cooked, poisoned, or, if lucky, just turned into frogs. Would my parents even recognize me as their son if I showed up on the doorstep croaking?

With the lights flickering and the eerie music playing, the chant ended, and the woman offered us each a cup of broth. We were too terrified to refuse. It had to be poisoned, and I wondered how my parents would ever be able to find my body in that strange house. These people would likely bury us in their backyard, and my parents would never find my body as we were far removed from our little street. I wasn't ready to die yet. Jack took a sip, and we waited for him to drop. I had already planned my escape through the curtain door; there had to be a back door. They might catch me, but I was going to die anyway. Jack suddenly looked up and said, "Wow, this is good! It's hot apple cider!" Stunned, I watched Frank pick up a cup and start drinking. Slowly, I lifted my cup and took a sip, which was delicious. Then out came some delicious cake, and any apprehensions soon faded. If this was poison, it certainly tasted great.

We soon learned that the woman and her husband were nearby Johns Hopkins University professors. We talked for a while and discovered that the group had gotten tired of strangers just coming by for candy. They wanted to interact with the kids, give them a real taste of Halloween, and get to know them a bit. They apologized for forgetting to turn on the light and were delighted that we had been brave enough to approach the door. They had wondered why no one else had shown up that evening and were thrilled that we could enjoy their food and hospitality. Suddenly the witches didn't look like witches at all.

What a fantastic end to a glorious evening. How sad that this could never happen today. Parents wouldn't let their kids go to a strange area alone, kids would be too fearful of going to a strange house, and the adults involved would somehow be accused of inappropriate behavior. It was one of the best Halloween scares I ever had. What is sad today is how the day has changed through the years. Scares now permeate the community about people hiding razor blades in apples or tainting candy somehow. Parents restrict or overprotect their kids, even going so far as to have the child's candy bag X-rayed. These incidents are extremely rare, but the rumors and fears of child predators take much of the fun and spontaneity out of the evening. Halloween was also supposed to be a child's day, although its original roots included adults. Today with all the commercial hyping, adults now indulge, and adult Halloween parties are prevalent; this bothers me as it should be a child's day. The day has also now been connected with several horror films involving some psychopathic slasher terrorizing a community or neighborhood. They require no imagination as the shock, blood, and gore are all too visible. Commercial haunted houses today are now patterned after the slash and gore movies. Sticking a hand into a bowl of spaghetti while in the dark or feeling grapes one was told were eyeballs have been replaced by an individual jumping out with a chainless chain saw to turn you into fish bait. That wonderful night years ago needed no slash and gore, simply the imagination of three young children who never should have ventured out of their neighborhood.

GOD DOESN'T UNDERSTAND THE EXPONENTIAL FUNCTION

At an early age, I learned that the exponential function would be my downfall. Led Zeppelin may have found the "Stairway to Heaven," but I had discovered the "Stairway to Hell." At the age of eight, I calculated over several nights that it was inevitable that I was going to hell. I honestly had tried to be a good kid, but there it was in black and white on the paper in front of me. I checked my math several times but arrived at the same results every time. There was no point in being a good kid anymore. It wasn't official yet, but my calculations were as straightforward as possible: I was going to Hell, and there was nothing I could do about it. My irrevocable reservation to Dante's Inferno had been placed.

I was raised by a devout Catholic mother and attended a Catholic school taught by cloistered nuns for the first three grades. The nuns were kind but certainly limited in their understanding of the world outside the walls of their convent. However, with the Almighty as their guide, they could keep us in line.

"God is everywhere and sees everything you do."

Even the bathroom was not safe from his gaze. In school, we memorized the Catholic catechism cover to cover, and these nuns and my mother had me thoroughly brainwashed at an early age. Many years later, those dreaded catechismal words are still etched in my brain:

1. Who made you? God made me. [Mom and Dad apparently had nothing to do with it.]
2. What else did God make? God made all things. [including this bloody catechism!]
3. Why did God make you and all things? For his glory. [That seems to make vanity a virtue.]
4. How can you glorify God? By loving him and doing what he commands. [My mother added a corollary to this: by doing what your mother commands.]

My mother was wonderful and loving, but religion ruled all. My siblings and I, however, would cringe when my mother pronounced, as she frequently did at the dinner table, that only Catholics went to heaven. At the other end of the table sat our Episcopalian father. We naturally deduced that he was going to Hell, the place which had been described to us by the nuns in such vivid detail that the description would have terrified even Dante. (Having watched enough marshmallows incinerate in a fire, I wondered how a person could roast for eternity.) Their terror tactics worked, however, as none of us dared step out of line. A better form of behavioral control never existed, but my sister and I did spend a lot of time figuring out how we could save my father. We even hung a crucifix above his bureau, figuring that when the angel of death came to get him, Dad might slip through the cracks, but then God knew and saw all. Didn't the Big Guy ever take a nap?

As a part of our early education, the nuns described the concept of sin to us in excruciating detail. This was a critical component of the brainwashing that must have inspired the Communists in the Korean War. (See *The Manchurian Candidate*.) There were both mortal and venial sins. We didn't sweat the venial sins because these wouldn't punch your ticket to hell. One would end up in Purgatory temporarily, roasting gently for a while, but one wasn't headed south for the ultimate weenie roast. However, mortal sins were a different story as even one of these would send you straight to hell if you died possessing one. Mostly we didn't sweat these deadly sins as we neither planned on murdering anyone nor coveting our neighbor's wife, not that an eight-year-old could even comprehend what that was. But unfortunately, stealing was on the list we were given, and by the age of seven, I had entered a life of crime. Beginning with taking a penny off my mother's bureau, I soon took small change from her purse.

My crime spree ended as my father caught on and set me up with a marked coin he left on his dresser, and I was ordered to go to confession to be absolved from my life of crime. My parents forgave me, and after getting the belt, which hurt far less than my parent's disappointment, I continued down the childhood path of a redeemed sinner. Realizing how close I had come to an all-expenses-paid vacation in the fires of hell, I completely changed my ways. The confession had erased the mortal sin of stealing, and I was again heaven-bound. However, my teacher let slip the ultimate bombshell, and I suddenly realized I was in real trouble.

The nun explained to the class that there was a wrinkle in the whole "confession erases the sin" deal. She explained that if one went to Communion without confessing a mortal sin, that act would be a mortal sin. Uh oh!! I had confessed the mortal sin of stealing, but, terrified of confronting the priest, I had let a week go by before confessing. Thus, I had been absolved of one mortal sin but unwittingly committed another since a Sunday with Communion had occurred in that interval. No problem, I just had to confess again for sin number two.

However, as I lay in bed one night, the reality of the predicament hit me like a ton of bricks. I had gone to Communion again before confessing the sin of taking Communion the week before without confessing. Thus, based on the nun's version of sin accumulation, I had committed a third sin, and this had not been confessed. Fifteen months had passed, and each Sunday, the unconfessed sins were adding up.

The way I had it figured, the following Sunday, I acquired a second sin for taking Communion for not confessing taking Communion the week before for not confessing. On the third Sunday, my sin total then rose to four as there were two sins not confessed when I took Communion. Each succeeding Sunday, each "unforgiven" sin was now doubling. For those not following, this is the warped mind of an eight-year-old child at work. My brain was now firing on all cylinders. I was frantic and jumped out of bed to do some serious math. I knew I was in deep doo-doo and realized I needed to sit down and calculate how many mortal sins I had committed over the 15 months since this all played out. That's when I first learned the power of the exponential function.

Most people are surprisingly ignorant of the exponential function, specifically what a doubling pattern can do. For example, if I begin with an empty container at 6 PM and every minute, the amount of water in it doubles, filling the container by midnight, at what time is the container half full? While many would quickly say 9 PM, the correct answer is 11:59 PM. While initially, the container remains virtually empty, that last doubling must take the container from half full to full. The other example I use is asking someone whether, if they worked for thirty days, would they rather be paid one thousand dollars a day or at a rate that doubled each day, beginning with a penny on day one (then two cents on day two, four cents on the third day, etc.). The one thousand dollars a day sounds like an obvious choice until one realizes that by doubling that initial one cent, on day thirty, you would receive over five million dollars for just that day alone.

I realized at age eight that my mortal sins were doubling every Sunday in that each unconfessed sin resulted in another mortal sin, thus doubling my accumulative sin total. Calculators did not exist for children in the 1950s, so I sat down with a pencil and a lot of paper to determine my fate. Using a calendar, I counted sixty-five Sundays since this bout of "sinning" had begun.

I began my chart:

Week	# Of Sins
1	1
2	2
3	4
4	8
5	16
6	32
7	64
8	128
9	256
10	512

Things were going downhill fast, and I had fifty-five more Sundays to get through. I passed one million sins on Sunday number twenty-one, and it only took until Sunday number thirty-one to pass one billion sins. I had some concept of large numbers as I had taken counting sheep to a whole new level, deciding that I would count to a million while lying in bed, waiting to fall asleep. I would count to one thousand and place a tally on the wall by my bed. I knew one thousand marks meant I had reached a million, and I invested a lot of bedtime in my venture. I finally quit at over 200,000, deciding that one million was … a humungous number. But a billion! That was a thousand of those millions I could never count to. The tallying continued as I realized that Dad would have company in hell. Would they allow us to play ball down there … or toss a fireball around?

The math continued; by the forty-first Sunday, I had reached one trillion sins, and by Sunday number fifty-one, it was time to get out the dictionary—I had passed the one "quadrillion" mark. Finally, I reached Sunday sixty-five, which I had just passed, and I was the not-so-proud owner of over 18,000,000,000,000,000.000 (eighteen quintillion) mortal sins. I was obviously in Guinness World Record territory and only eight. I could feel the heat from that subterranean oven already.

But wait! There was still the Confession Escape Clause. I just had to be forgiven for all of this before next Sunday. There was no way my mother would let me miss Communion, but I could feign sickness, miss church, and get a one-week extension. But how was I going to be forgiven for that many sins? How much time would it take? My eight-year-old mind was the master of math but seriously deficient in logic, and it never occurred to me that I could get lump absolution for my mountain of indiscretions. The mathematical exercise needed to continue as I had to find out how long it would take to confess eighteen quintillion sins—one at a time.

I timed myself and figured I could get one sin confessed in about fifteen seconds, thus clearing my slate of four sins a minute ... 240 an hour ... 5,760 in a twenty-four-hour period. This was getting depressing, and I was accumulating quite a pile of scrap paper on the floor. My parents had long since gone to sleep as I could no longer hear their TV downstairs. I finally calculated the critical figure—it would take around six trillion years to confess all these sins.

I was also an astronomy buff, so I had an idea how long the Earth would be here, and that answer was in the billions of years, not trillions. That intellectual pursuit also had a personal motivation. In case you didn't pick this up already, I am a worrier, and I had tossed and turned more than a few nights wondering if the Sun would come up the following day. My father assured me it would, but I needed better proof. I had found out that the Sun had enough fuel (hydrogen) to keep burning for several billion more years. I thought that if it was just up to God, he might forget one morning; this background information was very reassuring. In any event, there was no avoiding reality at this point—the Earth would not last long enough for me to confess all my sins; an eternity in Hell for me was a *mathematical certainty!*

I lay awake many nights after that fateful night of calculations, contemplating my fate. I had burnt my finger once, and that was just an exposure to fire for a couple of seconds ... but an eternity of roasting in a raging fire! I laugh now at the pathetic workings of that eight-year-old mind many years ago, but laughter was not part of my thoughts back then. Didn't God realize the mathematical impossibility he created? Had he done the math himself, he would have realized the predicament he put me in. And since it was impossible to confess, the sins continued to accumulate. My dictionary only included up to duodecillion (thirty-nine zeroes), and I soon knew I had flown by this number. I lost a lot of sleep that year and the year following. There was no way I would let someone know how deep in sin I now was. My mother still thought I was a good kid; if she only knew!

Both my father and mother have passed on at this point. All deceased humans must be down there with him if my father is burning in hell. OK, so I was a weird kid who took everything that was said to me to heart. My mother's intentions were honorable, and those poor nuns meant no harm. Times were different in the 1950s, but I lost a small chunk of my childhood by taking literally what I had been taught. I survived childhood, but I wish God had paid more attention in math class when they covered exponential functions.

THE CHRISTMAS PAINTING

Artistic ability should be in my DNA. My grandmother Radcliffe was an accomplished artist, painting portraits and landscapes. My father almost chose a career as an aeronautical engineer, and I remember looking at his intricate drawings of planes, landing systems, and wing designs. However, something went terribly wrong, as his child was artistically clueless. Had I been adopted? I liked to doodle, but my doodling was mostly just a collage of geometric patterns. I could draw a mean triangle, but I had difficulty drawing anything freeform, including stick figures. I was ten, in fifth grade, and an excellent student, at least until December of that year, when I received the dreaded assignment. We were to paint a Christmas painting to give to our parents. My initial reaction was a calm one as trees and presents were just geometric shapes, and with a good supply of red and green paint, I could master this as long as I could stick to two-dimensional objects. No problem!

I remember sitting in the art room that fateful day as Mrs. Murray outlined the assignment. She was a nice older woman, and this was the second year the poor soul had this artistic train wreck as a student. I had been a source of frustration for her, and I had overheard her talking to herself once as she walked away from me, the word "hopeless" clearly audible. I can't blame the woman; she spoke the truth. As she explained the project details, I confidently dreamed away of triangular trees and rectangular presents. I returned to the classroom upon hearing her utter my name. "George, you're going to paint the three wise men and their camels crossing the desert. We'll have this wonderful mural on the hallway wall when we put it all together. When you go home for Christmas, you can give your painting to your parents." Or at least that's what I thought she said; my brain had frozen on the words "the three wise men and their camels." How could one make people and camels out of triangles, squares, and rectangles? Even circles, which for me always became erratic ovals, would not help. And I had to paint this?

Depressed and bewildered, I went home that evening to get some advice from my father, the "artist." He had always drawn these characters for me, which he called "schmoes." His drawing consisted of a fence constructed of vertical boards with a "person" barely visible, his head protruding above the top of the fence, his fingers grasping the fence. He listened to my plight and promptly drew a "schmo" for me. From years of practice, he had gotten quite good at drawing these. What never occurred to the ten-year-old genius confronting him was that this was the only thing my father ever sketched, and it consisted almost entirely of geometric shapes. I've googled "schmo" and found nothing like my father's drawing. It must have been his creation, which did not catch on. I remember walking away from him that evening impressed with his "schmo" but simultaneously wondering how I could turn this into three wise men with their camels. I'm not sure there were many fences in the desert; even if there were, the wise men would not likely be hiding behind them. I was doomed. I was going to have to pull this off on my own.

I dreaded attending art class that day but was thrilled to find out a school assembly was going to preempt the class. I was no more prepared or confident when I slipped into my seat that second day. Everyone had their topic, and once the students got their eleven by seventeen-inch sheets of drawing paper and materials, the room erupted in a wave of creative excitement. I sat and stared at the paper, unsure how to begin. I could draw three stick figures, but how could you put a robe on a stick figure? I thought about the camels, and that was where panic set in. If I could have sketched a horse, I could have just added humps, but I had never actually drawn an animal before. I had attempted a dog once but soon realized it had a head bigger than its body and a severe case of elephantiasis of the legs. Panic quickly turned into depression, but I suddenly realized the paper was the same color as the sand in the desert. Wow, my painting was more than halfway done. Seeing the grin on my face, kindly Mrs. Murray came over to look over my shoulder. She quickly realized that her not-so-star pupil was in trouble. "Look," I said. "I've got the desert done." She laughed and then suddenly realized I wasn't joking.

I know Mrs. Murray had taught for many years and had encountered many "problem" students in all those years, but she was now having to redefine her definition of "problem." She was far from being my favorite teacher, but this was because this was the one class in which I could not excel. Digging into her vast reservoir of experience, she placed her hand on my shoulder, bent over, and whispered, "George, I can see you're having difficulty getting started, and most of the other students have completed their sketches. I'll make a deal with you. Work only on the three wise men this week, and I'll give you all of next week to work on the camels. We're doing a craft project next week, and I'll excuse you from that." With a small pat on my back, she walked on to the next person. She was as pleasant as any teacher, but I still had to draw and paint three people and three camels. A year would not have been a sufficient amount of time.

I sat there for a long time, just staring at the paper. This is a strategy that children sometimes employ—stare at a problem long enough, and it will soon go away or miraculously resolve itself. I had had a small degree of success with this, as my mother would quickly grow impatient and begin to help me out. If I had to clean up my room, I could sit on the bed and stare at the mess. Mom would soon come up to check on my progress, and so that she wouldn't have to come up and check on me a second time, she would begin to help out as I told her where each toy and book went. The only arena where this strategy failed was the dining room. I would stare at an inedible excuse for food, and it never once disappeared. However, staring at the "canvas" resulted in no sketch that day. The bell rang, and I instantly signed my name on the bottom corner of the paper. Day one completed.

I was a conscientious student and decided I would practice drawing a person at home. If I could master even part of it, that would give me a head start the next day. I was determined I could climb this mountain. I started drawing stick figures, figuring that would be a good starting point, but I soon realized that the arms and legs had to have joints, hands, and feet and that the head had to be more than just a little circle perched upon a vertical line. I started working on joints, but nothing I did seemed to model an actual elbow or knee. That's when my father climbed up to my room on the third floor to see how I was doing. I had been noticeably quiet at dinner that evening, so he knew something was amiss. I had been quiet that evening so no one would look over at me while secretly feeding my cauliflower to our dog. But he was correct; there was a massive weight on my mind, in the shape of three wise men and three camels. I explained the project I had been assigned, and he grabbed a piece of paper and a pencil and began to sketch. Five minutes later, I was staring at a drawing of six schmoes, three with two legs and the other three with four. I appreciated his caring and advice, but I was back to square one.

Somehow between that evening and the next day's art class, I built up my confidence. Kids can do that at times—become confident with no basis whatsoever. That's when we become the most dangerous, like when I thought I could disassemble Dad's portable radio and put it back together. I grabbed my "painting" from the pile, sharpened my pencil with the confidence of Rembrandt, and prepared to take off. I wasn't going to freeze today; I had to get started somehow. Even a lousy sketch was better than no sketch—or so I thought. I drew the stick figure I had "perfected" the previous evening. Now I just had to add some flesh to it, figuring it was doubtful the wise men were anorexic. My pencil work quickly went back and forth from pencil point to eraser, and soon I had a gaping hole in the paper. I was able to sneak another sheet of paper; shyness has its distinct advantages. I folded the original sheet, stuffing it in my pocket, to leave no evidence. The sketching continued, and the bell rang just as I had erased my stick figure for the third time on canvas number two. I wisely didn't put my name on the paper so dear old Mrs. Murray would not see my lack of progress. With a bit of luck, she would not notice that evening that there was no drawing of mine in the pile.

I decided that evening to block the whole subject out. I was often the caregiver for my little sister Kim when I got home from school. I took her to my room, and we built a castle for our stuffed bears, taking time off briefly for dinner, another meal our dog shared with me. Bedtime came, and I had completely forgotten about those cursed wise men. Why did they have to make that long journey anyway? If they hadn't followed that star, it surely would have simplified one child's life.

The next day was Thursday, and it suddenly dawned on me that I would have to have the wise men sketched AND PAINTED by the next day. There was no choice but to work fast. Perfection had to be cast to the wind, and I had to have the three figures sketched by the end of the period. Mrs. Murray, at this point, was busy with questions from the other kids, who knew what they were doing. Several parts of the mural were taking shape: shepherds standing in the snow with their sheep, colorful manger scenes, a bright star shining down on a stable, and Roman soldiers. I had a blank sheet of paper. There was no time to fret now; this was crunch time. I drew the stick figures, fleshed them out, and added eyes, ears, and noses. I remembered they needed crowns and gifts and quickly added a few geometric shapes.

The drawing was done. This wasn't going to hang in the Museum of Modern Art, but I finally could add a paper to the pile with more than my name on it. I walked out on top of the world. I had slain the art monster, and he was mine!

The next day would be a breeze. I had to add paint to my sketch, and since no one knew what the wise men looked like, I was free to be creative. I grabbed a set of watercolor paints and took off. Others were finishing, but many, like myself, were still painting. I wasn't even thinking about the camels I would have to draw; that was next week, and once the wise men were painted, it was the weekend, and NO SCHOOL! I watched the clock and finished with a whole five minutes to spare. That's when I saw Mrs. Murray walking my way. I didn't dread her visit this time because I had met my goal and tried my best. I didn't think she'd hold my painting up for the class to see, but I knew I would get a pat on the back. She walked around behind me and gazed down at my painting. She said nothing for an eternity, and I started to panic. Maybe she was trying to produce the right words for the praise due to me.

"That's good, George." There was an affirmation of my Herculean efforts. I hoped she remembered that I was to have an extra week to do the camels. She continued, "Next week, you're going to have to work on the three wise men." Had I heard her correctly? Was she looking at someone else's painting? "I'll help you get started on the three wise men on Monday." And she walked away! I was utterly shocked, but when I looked at my masterpiece, I could see it had flaws. I had sat in a corner, hoping to be unnoticed all week, but, more confident, was sitting out in the room today. A friend walked by, gazing at my painting, exclaiming, "What the heck is that?" I looked for a deep hole to climb into as three others ran over to see what had precipitated the comment. I quickly and correctly guessed that the soon-to-be-erected class mural would have no wise men as a part of it.

I've honestly blocked out the rest of the story. I know I completed that painting, but whether I drew three more wise men or attempted camels the next week has long been erased from this brain. I gave my parents the painting that Christmas, and, as only a mother could do, Mom told me it was the best Christmas present a mother had ever received. Up to that point, I had thought that my mother, a devout Catholic, always told the truth. To this day, I try to imagine my parents looking at that painting later that evening. I hear them saying, "What the heck is that?" Hey, but I got the desert right!

It's been several years since my mother passed away. No more loving mother ever existed, and her children were her life. In going through her massive collection of things she saved, I found poems and stories my siblings and I wrote, programs of school pageants, paintings, drawings, and projects we worked on. However, there was no Christmas painting from her eldest child in 1959. I don't fault her for that; I'm sure it had a message saying, "This painting will self-destruct in five seconds." And the world is undoubtedly a better place for this. Mrs. Murray should have been given a purple heart for having to teach me, and my artistic career has only gone downhill since then. The advent of computers was manna from heaven for this individual, and I soon became the master of "copy and paste." All the players in this artistic tragedy have passed, save me, and when I share the story, people always laugh at the punch line, "And next week you can do the three wise men." They, of course, think the whole story is fabricated, but up in heaven somewhere, there is an art teacher who knows better. She looks back on her lengthy career with a smile, but she remembers the one blemish on her career. "How in the world could one of my students draw a person who looked like a camel?"

THE DREADED SPHERES
FROM HELL

I glanced up at the clock... 8:30 PM, and I was sore from sitting so long in the kitchen chair; the others had gone up to watch TV a couple of hours ago. I had been alone in the kitchen for so long that I wondered if it were, in fact, 8:30 AM. And there they were ... still sitting on my plate, staring back at me. Those dreaded little green spheres had not budged an inch. And I was supposed to eat them? This certainly bordered on child abuse. This wasn't food; these were Brussels sprouts, a premier form of child torture.

History says that they originated in Ancient Rome; no wonder the Roman Empire fell. Who needed the Goths and Huns? These little monstrosities could bring down any civilization. They were all the reason I needed to avoid the city of Brussels, and who was the sadistic botanist who brought them into this country anyway? Where was the Department of Home Security when we needed it?

"Do not leave this table until you have cleared your plate!" sounded my parents. Arguing would be futile with a stubborn mother and a father who was a crackerjack trial lawyer. After a lecture about how my mother survived the Depression when no one ever left anything behind on a plate, my parents went to another room. Curse the Depression; that was thirty years ago! My brain was already churning away even before they left the room; there had to be a better way to remove these vile objects rather than consume them. This ritual sadly had played out several times before, but never with a happy conclusion. But children are eternally hopeful.

After two hours, the Brussels sprouts hadn't moved; maybe they would start to evaporate or decompose if I waited long enough. Entropy was a fundamental principle of physics, but it doesn't apply to Brussels sprouts. An hour earlier, I had tried to force part of one down but had gagged it onto my plate. I was not proud of this pathetic performance, but I could not force these little cannonballs down. Desperation was setting in now. When they found my body several days later, starvation would be all that would show up in the autopsy. My parents would not be implicated in the crime. What had I done to turn them against me? I was a good son, so why were they subjecting me to this torture?

Usual means of food removal were useless here. Nickie, the world's fattest beagle, had spit one out a couple of months before. This dog consumed everything in sight but wanted nothing to do with these little green time bombs. Because of their solid spherical nature, it was impossible to hide them under the centerpiece to be removed at a later time. This strategy worked for every other food item, as my sister and I had hidden enough food there to feed an entire country. It's incredible how much sauerkraut one can fit under a bowl of fruit. One could always wrap unwanted food in a napkin, but the shape and volume of Brussels sprouts prohibited this. A desperate race to the bathroom with a mouth full of them was futile because I would have to pass by "the sentinel," who would undoubtedly ask me a question. Ever try talking with a mouth full of Brussels sprouts? Demosthenes should have tried these instead of marbles. So, the little green bowling balls just sat on the plate. Why did I think time would supply a solution? Would I eventually be excused from the table? The two hours which had elapsed so far answered that question. It is a characteristic of young children to procrastinate the inevitable. The adult mind so easily perceives that quickly addressing the issue is the best course, but the child stays forever hopeful. However, the only thing worse than a Brussels sprout is a cold, now dried-out Brussels sprout.

The litany of adult admonitions continued to race through my mind:

"Eat them; they're good for you!" - And so is an enema!

"Eat these, and you can have dessert." - Forget dessert; I had a candy bar in my room.

"But your sister likes them." - What boy wants to be like his younger sister? And she didn't like them!

"They'll taste better if you eat them while they're hot." It was already too late for that.

"Try them; you might like them." - Fat chance! Did any kid buy that line? I wasn't just some little ignorant child; I was nine years old!

"Everybody likes Brussels sprouts." - Oh, right! What about Nickie? And we all like being dipped in boiling oil, too!

"People in Africa are starving." – You know my response to that one – "so pack them up and send them to Africa. I'll happily pay the postage."

No use. They continued to sit on my plate. *Leave It to Beaver* was about to come on the TV, my last chance to see a show before bedtime. Nickie wandered through the room, looking for scraps of food. When she wasn't sleeping, her activity for twenty-three hours each day, she searched the environs for a missed crumb or two. She was a beagle, and no crumb escaped her nose for long. She liked food; whole turkeys had disappeared in her presence. Maybe I would try Nickie again; it was still the best possibility. I reached down to pet her, but with her first look at the spherical toxin, she sprinted out of the room, tail between her legs.

Then an inspiration! The window! Waiting until my mother was temporarily out of sight, I carefully crept across the room and raised the screen, tossing the first Brussels sprout into the yard. Now I could use my spoon as a catapult from my seat. Soon number two was flying out the window. The victory was in sight. As I was ready to launch the last evil projectile toward the window, my mother suddenly walked into the room. "Great, you only have one left."

"Gee, Mom, since there's only one left, can I leave it and go?"

"Well, since you were able to eat five, eating one more should be no problem. Just pop it in, and you'll be done." It sounded so easy, but these were BRUSSELS SPROUTS!

Knowing I only had one to eat, I summoned the courage that had failed me the last two hours and popped the toxic pill in. Holding one's nose minimizes the taste slightly, but it doesn't work with Brussels sprouts. I didn't remember swallowing the darn thing, but I remember it coming back up … with the partially digested residue of my dinner.

"Oh honey," Mom said. "That's so silly. Anyone can eat without getting sick. Act more grown-up next time." But I didn't hear a word she said as I was racing toward the TV. I entered the family room just in time to see the closing credits rolling off the screen. There would be no show tonight—those danged Brussels sprouts.

❖ ❖ ❖

With age comes wisdom, supposedly. My children were sometimes forced to eat things they didn't want, but I remember swearing that I would never force them to eat Brussels sprouts. While they weren't subjected to those poison pills, my son still claims he can't drink orange juice because he was forced to drink it as a child. Why do parents try to inflict on their children what they know from their experience doesn't work? Revenge on an innocent victim? Or now that roles are reversed, do we think this is part of the adult agenda?

I still stay far away from Brussels sprouts—too much water under the bridge here. My children have done a much better job getting their children to eat. I loved my mother, but cooking was not her forte, contributing to my eating "disorder." My maternal grandmother was a great Southern cook, and I spent considerable time in her home. I lived for her breakfasts, quite different from the cold, lumpy oatmeal that often frequented our table at home.

I'm an adult now; at least that's what my driver's license says. I haven't had to eat a Brussels sprout in almost 60 years, and I am thus possibly the happiest person on Planet Earth. I've led a relatively sheltered life and traveled little. My military experience consisted of braving the Baltimore Beltway for a brief period. My Uncle Teddy was a prisoner of war in Germany during World War II, and I often think of the torture he had to endure. Would I be strong enough to resist what he must have experienced? Starvation—I could manage it. Brainwashing—I am pretty strong-willed. Pain—I could put up with a lot. But Brussels sprouts? I'd tell all!

TAKING MY DOG TO SCHOOL

Every child should have a dog, the required equipment for surviving childhood, and a beagle is the best dog a child can have. I am, of course, just a wee bit biased in this regard as I can define the stages of my life by the beagles I have owned (although beagles actually own you). A more stubborn breed has never existed, but they are a pure blend of unconditional devotion and non-stop entertainment. My first beagle was Nickie, named ever so creatively for the ... nick in her ear. She was not my first dog but a replacement for a mutt we had gotten a year earlier.

As an eight-year-old, I had never had a dog, a surprising fact considering that the antics of my father's childhood dogs frequently made it into our dinnertime conversation. My mother was not a dog person, actually not a pet person of any kind. Knowing that any dog would be Mom's responsibility most of each weekday, Dad wisely refrained from adding to our family. All of that changed at a small school bazaar at my grade school while I was in third grade. That day a small puppy was up for adoption. A scrawny mutt, if ever there was one, immediately attracted my attention. My pleas to have Mom take it home were ignored. I rolled out every argument imaginable:

"I'll take care of it." (I couldn't even keep my room clean.)

"We need a watchdog." (The puppy might have defended us from a butterfly.)

"It needs a good home." (That line would surely work.)

"I'll do even more chores around the house if I have a dog to help." (And pigs fly!)

And the ultimate child's argument, "It won't be any trouble because it can sleep in my room."

But this was not to be. Even a good bout of crying with my sister sobbing in harmony failed to move my mother. We were not going to have a dog. That night I cried myself to sleep. The tears for my mother earlier in the day had been a carefully orchestrated performance, but these were now genuine; something about that sad-looking puppy had touched me, and I would never be the same again.

To make matters worse, the family who adopted the dog lived on our narrow little street. The puppy now belonged to my brother's friend, so I saw it frequently. "Why couldn't it have been mine?" About a month later, I was up at the boy's house with my brother when his mother told us they could not keep the dog; would we be interested? My feet never hit the pavement as I raced home. It never occurred to me that my request had been denied once already; hope springs eternal in the mind of an eight-year-old boy. After the third or fourth "no," it was time to bring on the tears again, but to no avail. I didn't know how long I could keep up the act, but I was determined to get the dog this time.

After over an hour of trying to force out tears, I made no headway. My father entered the front door at that point, and I could hear a heated conversation downstairs. I listened but could only hear the murmur of the two talking. Before I could recharge for another round of crying, I heard Dad's footsteps heading up my way. He walked into my room.

"So, I hear you want this puppy."

I launched into my litany of reasons why this would be the best decision the family could ever make, but he stopped me before I could even get to reason number three. The smile on his face told me that our family would get a dog. Victory! After a brief walk up the street and a short conversation with the neighbor, we were soon heading back with Friskie, the world's ugliest puppy. Thus began a love affair to last a lifetime. I would now never be complete without a four-legged friend beside me.

Sadly, a year later, we discovered the dog was deaf, and my parents said she was taken to the country where she would be safer. Unbeknownst to me, Friskie had been put to sleep, and when I discovered several years later that I had been duped, I was furious. Protecting a child from reality is not always the best plan, particularly when it appears to the child to be a lie. However, within twenty-four hours, we went out to find a replacement dog, and Nickie, a six-month-old beagle, was the first and only dog we looked at. My father explained that we might want to look at some beagle puppies, but Nickie and I had already bonded. Little did I know how that dog would begin to work its magic. Nickie and I became inseparable.

By age eleven, we had just moved into a new house, and I had left all my friends behind in the previous neighborhood. But who needs friends if you have a beagle? Nickie followed me everywhere. This was a wonderful time when dogs did not need to be confined or on a leash. It didn't take her long to acquire the typical beagle figure, but she could still keep up with ease as I walked and biked through our section of the city. I walked three-quarters of a mile to school, and Nickie would usually trot along beside me. We had to cross one of the major intersections in Baltimore, but Nickie would follow me across. A young female traffic police officer helped control the car and pedestrian traffic at the light. Nickie invariably would trot up behind the police officer and lick her hand. The poor woman would scream and throw both her hands in the air causing the cars to screech to a halt, horns blowing. Nickie and I would continue across the street, pretending not to know what was happening. This scene repeated itself innumerable mornings, much to my delight. She would stop at the school property boundary, and as I walked off, she would then make her long trek home, stopping, as I later found out, at the local butcher shop for a bone. She and I had the routine down to a science.

That dog was my life. Nickie would sit on the porch each afternoon when I arrived home, follow me upstairs while I did my homework, and then accompany me out to play. By age twelve, I was never without that plump ball of brown, black, and white fur trailing behind me. Beagles make great pets for many reasons; one gets two dogs for the price of one. Not only does one get a wonderful and adaptable indoor pet, but also a veritable three-ring circus when the dog goes outside. In addition to the lovable companion, a beagle is a howling banshee and the original Sherlock Holmes, inquisitively searching out every smell—endless entertainment and one comedic escapade after another. And Nickie was a true-blue beagle.

It was in sixth grade that my most memorable day ever in school occurred. Nickie made the usual walk to school with me, terrorizing the poor police officer once again, disrupting all traffic flow, and as usual, stopped at the edge of the school property. She waited until I walked off toward the buildings and began her trot home. That morning we had an assembly at the school. A friend and I had done an excellent job of not paying attention to what was happening. Bored, I had taught him Morse Code, and we were tapping messages back and forth instead of listening to the speaker. I had no clue what the assembly was about that day, but I was to remember that assembly forever.

Our "conversation" was interrupted by squeals on the other side of the auditorium. Students were jumping up in sequence much as crowds now do in a stadium when doing the wave. I was in the next to last row in the large auditorium, but I could see what was happening up front. The speaker had stopped, and the students kept jumping up, the waves moving across the rows and gradually toward the back of the auditorium. The teachers tried futilely to get the students back in their seats so our speaker could continue. This was great, something to break up the monotony of the day, but no one near me could figure out exactly what was going on. A mouse? That made no sense since a mouse wouldn't be causing all the laughter filling the room. The "wave" got closer and closer to me until suddenly, from out below the seat in front of me appeared ... Nickie. At this point, all decorum in the assembly was lost, and I was asked to escort my dog out of the assembly to the applause of most of my classmates. The teachers were not pleased.

I carried her outside, instructing her to go home as I did each morning. She wagged her tail and smiled. Beagles do smile, and I knew I had the most intelligent dog in the world. I gave her an extra head scratch and hug and headed back into the auditorium. The speaker had restarted his talk, and I was both embarrassed and pleased. I was the shy kid who no one noticed, but every student stared at me as I walked back to my seat. Nickie had briefly made me the star. My friend and I returned to our "conversation," stopping only when the applause erupted after the speaker finished. We joined in, utterly clueless as to what we were applauding.

It was time to file out of the auditorium and walk back to class. Looking at my watch, I realized the assembly hadn't lasted long enough to postpone the history quiz I had not studied enough for. Was Franklin Pierce the thirteenth or fourteenth President? My thoughts were suddenly interrupted by my "friend" weaving through the crowd to find me. Nickie was still here and had checked each person in the lengthy line to find me. She filed into our class line unbeknownst to my teacher, so I pretended not to notice. Nickie followed us right into the classroom and moved under my desk. Could I get away with this? Like a good student, I picked up my pencil and went to work, scratching the dog's head with my left hand. Eventually, Mr. H heard a little commotion and came over to my desk. At this point, he did something that made him a favorite teacher. He leaned down, scratched her head, and said, "Welcome to sixth grade." That would be the first of several times that year that Nickie attended school. For a kid that didn't quite feel a part of things, I felt on top of the world. Nickie had made me a temporary star of the class.

I shared my lunch with her that day, and she joined us on the playground. She slept under my desk all afternoon, and when it came time to walk home, I now had someone to accompany me. She had become quite the hit that day, and everyone had to bid her goodbye. What a triumphant walk home from school that was. My dog had gone to school and spent the entire day with me. I might even like school if I could be accompanied by a dog daily. I had to leave her behind when I walked to school the next few days, but about a week later, she showed up at my classroom door again. Once again, she spent the day under my desk, bringing many smiles to some young faces.

It was a glorious year, the happiest of my school career. With Nickie appearing from time to time, I felt safe and noticed. People in the community knew that if they saw me, Nickie would be trailing right behind. She was my best friend, always accepting, never judgmental, and eternally faithful. Toward the end of the school year, her appearances in school had tapered off, but when I got home, she was always sitting on the porch when I rounded the corner. She would race out to see me, and the books would hit the ground as I sat down to play with her, rubbing her belly and rolling with her in the grass. We'd then run to the house with Nickie struggling to keep up. Beagles are built for noise, not speed.

Early the next school year, I arrived home from school and was surprised when I did not see her on the porch. Figuring that my mother had failed to put her outside, I raced into the house to look for her. There wasn't the usual bark and pitter-patter of feet. Possibly she had been taken to the vet, but then Mom's car was outside. Confused, I walked into the kitchen only to see a white sheet covering something on the floor. Terror spread through me as my imagination started filling in the blanks. Lifting the sheet, I suddenly died. Nickie lay there motionless with some dried blood beside her on the floor. I went into shock and barely noticed my mother entering the room.

"George, I'm sorry; she was hit by a car this afternoon. But we can get another dog."

I barely heard her as I stared at my best friend lying on the floor. Someone had brought the dog into the house and put it there on the kitchen floor, and Mom was waiting for Dad to get home. She tried to comfort me, but a hug doesn't register when your entire world has just ended. I covered Nickie up and just sat down in the corner. The tears flowed and flowed and flowed. I had never experienced death before and had no tools to deal with what I was feeling. Surely this would pass, and Nickie would be there to greet me tomorrow. This couldn't be the end. I was utterly devastated.

I vaguely remember my father walking in soon after, and I could hear them talking in the hallway. All I could do was look at that lump under the sheet, hoping that this would all pass, and I would start to see the sheet move. My father walked in and didn't know what to say. I knew he knew what I was feeling, however. Mom told me it was time to act more like an adult and stop crying. I'll never forget her next words, "It's just a dog." Anger now flew into me; this was more than a dog. Nickie had become my life, my constant companion, my joy. And she was never coming back! The crying continued well into the evening until I was drained and almost devoid of feeling. Then followed one of the longest nights of my life and the longest school day I have ever endured. I didn't want to talk, I couldn't concentrate, and my smile was gone. I half expected to hear that bark when I returned home that day, to see her race out to greet me, tail wagging incessantly. My life changed forever. To this day, that death is the most challenging tragedy I have endured. Other losses were more severe, but unprepared as I was for death, that loss completely crushed me.

Within a week, Dad and I traveled to the country to look for another beagle. Once again, we only looked at one. Eight-week-old

Dixie looked up at me once, and the search was over. Another beagle hijacked my heart, but I never forgot Nickie. People say losing a dog is easier than losing a human because you can replace a dog, but there was no replacement for Nickie. She had changed me forever and gotten me through a couple of tough years. Dixie would become an incredible pet and companion, but she was never a replacement. I still remember Nickie snoring under my desk in school and that marvelous teacher who allowed it to happen. He was a wise man, knowing that this was more than just a dog to that awkward twelve-year-old. As I said, beagles define the stages of my life, and Nickie marked the end of my childhood. While I had learned how cruel life could be, I also experienced the joy of companionship and unconditional love.

SPAM IN A CAN*

It was early morning on May 5, 1961, and sixth-grade schoolwork was not the primary thing on my mind. Arithmetic, spelling, and geography did little to sustain my interest, but current events that year made life exciting. We had a new young President in John F. Kennedy, someone a kid could identify with, but the world was becoming a more frightening place with trouble next door in Cuba and the erection of the Berlin Wall. In contrast to the fear of the Cold War, the music scene was anything but serious, with rock still in its infancy, everyone doing the Twist, and the Beach Boys and Motown just getting started. The country was beginning to celebrate the centennial of the Civil War, bringing history to life for this twelve-year-old kid. Still, the exploration of space was what captured my attention and imagination. That day was going to be a day to top all days as the United States was finally going to launch a man into space.

The anticipated space launch had been delayed multiple times by malfunctions and disasters, but it was finally here. Even though the Russians had beaten us a month earlier to the coveted prize of being the first when Yuri Gagarin was launched into a one-orbit flight, this was the day I had anticipated for a good portion of my young life. At the height of the Cold War, to this young kid from Baltimore, beating the Russians was even better than the Orioles beating the

* The term "spam in a can" was used by early astronauts to refer to the early manned space capsules. Tom Wolfe used the term in his book, *The Right Stuff*, and it is often attributed to test pilot Chuck Yeager.

Yankees. The seven Mercury astronauts had been selected two years earlier, and Alan Shepard had been chosen to make the first flight. These seven were the superheroes of our generation, easily surpassing Brooks Robinson, Willie Mays, and Johnny Unitas. We dreamed of standing in their shoes one day and simulated our ride into space. Shepard was to ride in a capsule launched by a Redstone rocket from Cape Canaveral in Florida (later renamed Cape Kennedy). He had named his capsule Freedom 7, with the seven standing for the seven astronauts in the program.

I got up early that day to watch the countdown and launch on TV, hoping I would have time to see it before leaving for school. As I sat at the TV set watching the countdown. I was as excited as a kid on Christmas morning but also scared. From the late 1950s until this point, the U.S. space program had its share of disasters: crashes and rockets blowing up on the launch pads. And now we were going to put a human on top of this towering powder keg and "light the candle," as the astronauts referred to the ignition. The launch was scheduled for around 7:30 AM, giving me time to watch the short flight and then make the three-quarter-mile walk to school. The flight was delayed again, with a few minutes left in the countdown. I would now have to race to school and hopefully find some way of watching or listening to the flight.

I ran up Roland Avenue as fast as I could. My beagle Nickie, who usually made the walk to school with me, gave up and headed home early. I arrived at school only to find the flight was still delayed. The classroom had no TV or radio, but our teacher assured us we would get to a radio somehow. He had snuck a radio into the classroom for the World Series in the fall, and we knew he'd come through for us. The launch had been pushed back numerous times through early 1961, and our manned space flight program seemed doomed. A couple of months earlier, Ham had been the first primate to go into space. The chimp had made the cover of Life Magazine, but the real excitement would be the launch of a human. Ham's capsule had severely overshot the anticipated touchdown location, and he had come close to drowning. However, when they opened the capsule and presented him with an apple, he was as happy as a ... chimp. The problems with his flight only added to the concerns over a human flight. The capsule was tiny at best, with the astronaut doing little flying. Test pilot Chuck Yeager had referred to this human-crewed capsule as "spam in a can." All of this added to the tension which built up before the flight. There were so many things that could go wrong, most of all the re-entry, where the capsule heated up to thousands of degrees, with the astronauts protected by a heat shield that "might" work. It was too easy for the vivid imaginations of eleven and twelve-year-old kids to picture the "spam" seriously overcooking.

Shortly after school started, NASA resumed the countdown, and all the students in the older grades were ushered into the music room in the school. There was one tiny radio plugged in at the front of the room, and we strained to hear the countdown report. Every student was sitting on the edge of their seat; there were no attention span issues that morning. NASA went into a short mandatory hold with a few minutes remaining, and we all groaned. Shepard had already been sitting cramped in this tiny capsule for four hours, which was no exaggeration since any movement was impossible. And what would happen if he had to go to the bathroom? We found out later that this was an issue with, unfortunately, only one solution.

This last delay was a dirty trick to play on young kids; forget that it was a necessary safeguard built into every flight. We couldn't stand the suspense. The countdown resumed, and we grew terrified when the count went below a minute. That was one long minute, and we finally got to 10, 9, 8, 7, 6, 5, 4, 3, 2, 1, ignition ... blast off. It was 9:34 AM, and the decisive moment had finally arrived. In today's world, where we watch all on TV, it's hard to describe listening to the event. In those days, even on TV, one could only follow the rocket visually for the first few seconds, and then it became a primarily audio event. We had seen enough rocket launches to picture what was happening. I remember holding my breath and praying we wouldn't hear a report of an explosion or the rocket suddenly veering off course. The astronaut could blow the hatch on the capsule and eject, but there was some question as to whether this would even work. As the seconds passed, all sounded AOK. We could follow the dialogue as the mission control crew talked to Shepard. As the rocket soared higher and higher into space, we cheered heartily. Our hero was doing it! We all knew, however, that the take-off was only obstacle number one. Skeptics had made his chances of surviving the flight slim, and we were scared.

The rocket fell away from the capsule, and the capsule continued its ascent. This was not going to be an orbital flight. The capsule would reach an apogee and then fall back to Earth, the space equivalent of throwing a rock up in the air and having it land in a pond. Future flights would put the capsule in orbit. This flight and the one to follow would test the rocket launch and capsule recovery. The flight was only projected to go fifteen minutes, and never did fifteen minutes seem so long. The capsule made it up over 100 miles and began its fall back to Earth. Soon came the dreaded communications blackout as the capsule heated up from friction while re-entering the atmosphere, No one in the room made a sound as Shepard could no longer be heard. As the minutes passed, our imaginations again started painting the worst-case scenario. Finally, we could hear his voice again, and the cheer that went up was much louder than the one that followed the take-off.

He splashed down in the Atlantic close to the planned target area, and soon a helicopter had the capsule in sight. There still was incredible tension as there was the possibility of the capsule sinking. This did happen on the second manned flight, but fortunately, the astronaut Gus Grissom was able to get out. Soon the chopper had the capsule on a cable and was carrying it toward the ship. The cheers erupted again when the capsule was finally placed on the aircraft carrier. The Orioles winning the World Series on a ninth-inning home run would not have been as exciting. Shepard was instantly a national hero, getting to meet President Kennedy and getting a fantastic ticker tape parade through New York City with tons of confetti raining down on him. The moon landing eight years later was amazing but not as tense as that simple fifteen-minute loop into space.

This was a time of real heroes, much to inspire a young boy. Of course, the original astronauts were all male and white. The world wasn't ready for a female to risk her life, and we were still quite far from racial equality. The astronauts were all top fighter pilots, and blacks were just starting to ascend into this stratosphere of piloting. These pilots were true daredevils. Several years later, while in the Air Force, I was at a base when Deke Slacum, one of the Mercury 7, flew in. I remember his take-off. He put the nose of the plane up at what almost seemed a vertical angle and disappeared quickly into the clouds. It was amazing. Our heroes today are usually athletes and music stars, but our heroes in the 1960s were accomplishing something significant for our country. So much was learned from these early flights and the later Gemini flights (two men in a capsule), followed by the Apollo flights, which eventually took us to the Moon. Computer technology arrived years earlier because of these missions. There had been giant computers before, but they needed to be tremendously reduced in size for these flights. Even with the Cold War, this was a golden age for the country.

On November 12, 2014, the European Space Agency landed a robot on a comet after chasing it through the Solar System for ten years. This is technologically amazing and makes "throwing" Shepard up in the air for fifteen minutes seem almost silly. There was minimal news coverage of today's rendezvous, but not the considerable build-up that each Mercury, Gemini, and Apollo flight had. CNN covered the landing, but no one would have thought to bypass their beloved soap operas for the event. In the 1960s, all programming ceased, and virtually all work stopped for those flights. Granted, with today's event, there was not the drama that comes from having a human on board, but the event went mostly unnoticed. How sad! We've become so complacent about space exploration, and NASA's budget is a fraction of what it used to be. In the 1960s, the plan was to land a man on Mars by the 1990s; now, I doubt it will happen in my lifetime.

It's sad today that children don't have the type of heroes we had. It's hard for me to think of a highly-paid athlete as a hero. Our nation has had its share of heroes as we established and explored our country, survived terrible wars, and made many technological discoveries, all of which made modern life possible in this country. Few today remember Alan Shepard, and space flight seems mundane to the average child as Star Wars and Star Trek are more likely to capture a child's imagination. Space flight is still dangerous, but nothing compared to those earliest flights. Chuck Yeager was always a hero to many as he was the first to break the sound barrier, an event many skeptics predicted would destroy his plane. He lacked the academic and service background to be one of the original seven astronauts, but his daring flights paved the way for manned space flight. Yeager and these early astronauts risked their lives to make today's space program possible. It was a different time, and few my age will ever forget the drama that unfolded on May 5, 1961, a day that fueled one young boy's dreams.

ACROPHOBIA BLUES

The child stood terrified on the edge of a thirty-foot-high bridge above West Canada Creek in Upper New York State. He had been coaxed into jumping by his peers, and without thinking, he had climbed through the railing onto a narrow girder about a foot below the level of the road. He was holding onto the railing, facing away from the bridge, and was now looking down for the first time. Thirty feet from below didn't seem so high as he had been sitting down there watching others jump off, screaming as they dropped to the deep water below, but now looking down, the thirty feet seemed to have grown to 100. What had possessed him to climb out here? He was terrified of heights and now stood with thirty feet between him and impact. He heard the voices in his head. "From a great height, hitting the water is like dropping on concrete!" "Keep your legs firmly together, or you'll sing soprano for the rest of your life!" The other kids were now starting to chant, "Jump! Jump! Jump!" But there was no way he was going to jump. He began concocting an excuse for backing out. Dizzy spell? Nausea? Need to defecate? How about a cramp? They'd have to buy that one. He called back to the group, mentioning his growing cramp. But in return, he only heard, "Jump! Jump! Jump!" He wasn't even sure he could climb back off this girder onto the bridge, but there would be no jump. The seconds turned to minutes, and the water was receding from view. He was in real trouble! The cries for him to jump continued, but fear made the sounds seem to fade. He searched desperately for a way out of his predicament but was too frightened to think.

58 Years Later:

Yes, I am afraid of heights; there's no denying that, but my acrophobia is well-rooted. A phobia is an unrealistic fear of something, but the last time I checked, there was this force called gravity, which was very real. Gravity had not always been my friend. I somehow managed to fall down a complete set of stairs at an early age but learned my lesson at age seven when a friend and I decided to sumo wrestle on top of a table. I lost, or more accurately, my collarbone lost. The laws of physics also dictate that one will accelerate as one falls, thus impacting the ground at a higher velocity if falling from a greater height. After those early disasters, I decided not to become a physics demonstration. My apprehension with heights seems to be more of a mathematical issue than a phobia. My odds of staying alive decreased as the height above the ground increased.

Now there is nothing more wonderful than a view from a high place. There is something exhilarating about standing at an overlook on a mountain; one gets a unique perspective on our surroundings. Just don't make me get near the edge. There is also a physiological basis for my fear: poor balance. When trying to cross a stream on a log, I was the kid who would fall in. I finally just learned to walk through the stream; I emerged much less wet that way. If the police ever pull me over at a sobriety checkpoint and make me walk a straight line, I would be locked up for sure. The blood test would affirm my sobriety, but I can't walk a straight line without wobbling to the side once or twice. My doctor is aware of my lack of balance and wants to run a series of tests. He's about sixty-five years too late.

I have an advanced degree in stumbling. I have scars on my knees to prove it, and the knees of all my pants have grass stains and tears.

I fall all the time, much to everyone's horror, but I never hurt myself. But put me up high, and the fall won't be as fun. Ladders frighten me, but I've got my hands for added support there. I don't do roofs and have a grab bar in my shower. So, is this a phobia, or is it just being smart? I always play the odds, which is why I don't buy lottery tickets, and extreme height is a lottery ticket I'm definitely passing on.

Now I may have missed out on a lot as a kid, and that upper arm strength I could have developed while climbing never materialized. My ancestors may have originated in the trees, but I must have alien DNA. You will never see this part-Irish individual kissing the Blarney Stone, and I don't have to worry about rock climbing on the completely flat terrain of Dorchester County, Maryland. All the primate DNA must have made it to my sister Gussie, who was fearless, spending a good portion of her childhood in trees.

When one has an unrealistic fear, it is best to confront it head-on. I failed this therapy as a child, avoiding any place higher than three or four feet. I avoided roller coasters and tall ladders. My father had an office some twenty stories up in Baltimore, and I did like the view, but then the windows were closed, and I reasoned that the building was not going to topple. I did learn to dive off a diving board, reasoning that water was not hard, but no one was getting me up on a high dive. All of this changed when I was thirteen.

The summer of 1963 was my second year at a remarkable boys' camp in Upper New York State. My home had become stressful, and my father had wisely talked me into attending a residential camp the year before. Homesickness had disappeared within twenty-four hours that first summer as I quickly immersed myself in canoeing, sailing, archery, and a series of incredible camping trips. Hyde Bay Camp had a unique philosophy: never force any child to do anything except eat, sleep, and pass a minimum swimming test. The camp, run by a Harvard professor, had thrived for thirty-five years before I entered the scene. Despite the unusual philosophy, the camp was a beehive of activity. The occasional kid would sit in his tent wanting to do nothing but read comic books, but the subtle coercion of counselors and peers would soon have the child deep in some activity. The schedule each day was one that each camper designed themselves. The bottom line was that it worked.

Hyde Bay Camp was situated on Otsego Lake near Cooperstown, NY. I would have been lost at a traditional camp with a regimented schedule. I thrived on the freedom to learn and explore at my own pace. As a shy kid, I would have been lost in the ebb and flow of a rigid camp routine, but at Hyde Bay, I could find myself at a comfortable pace. Every child was made to feel unique and essential, and the abundant creativity and humor that pervaded all activities made for highly memorable moments. It was here that the kid, who had grown up in a row house in the city, discovered the natural world: sleeping all summer in a tent, hiking, canoeing, and exploring.

This second summer, I opted for two months, thriving in this non-pressure environment. I had passed Junior Life Saving and now qualified for the ultimate trip, the one I had heard described in a myriad of stories since my first day at the camp—the Trenton Falls trip. Trenton Falls was an impressive waterfall along West Canada Creek, which emptied into the Mohawk River. The trip was a wonderful three days full of swimming, hiking, camping, and canoeing. The first day was a day of swimming in Ohio Gorge, the second was a climb down into Trenton Falls itself for a day of skinny dipping, since the area was isolated and always devoid of human life, and the third day was a wild day of white water canoeing down West Canada Creek. This was heaven for a kid who had grown up in the city. I had dreamed about this trip but knew I had to pass the prerequisite requirements to qualify: Junior Life Saving and a canoeing test. The canoeing test was easily mastered the first summer. Despite being a below-average swimmer, I successfully toughed out the lifesaving course in the first month of that second summer,

One piece of the trip was part of every recounting of past trips: jumping off a thirty-foot bridge into the creek below. But this had not concerned me since I kept reminding myself of the camp philosophy that one could choose to do or not do every activity. This was a simple decision; I was not going to jump off the bridge, and since two of my friends also planned to be non-jumpers, I would be in good company. The first morning of swimming at Ohio Gorge was spectacular—small waterfalls with nice low ledges to jump from for an intoxicatingly wonderful time. After lunch, we were transported to another swimming spot where the fun would continue. We swam around the bend, and suddenly there it was—the bridge. My heart sank, but I kept reminding myself that jumping was 100% optional.

The counselors checked the water depth below the bridge, and not one could even find the bottom. The jumping could commence. Several counselors took turns making the plunge, and one even climbed up on the suspension girders, diving in from about fifty feet up. It was a great show from my vantage point down at water level. They then instructed us on proper technique, the most crucial point of which was to keep our legs together as we hit the water for obvious testicular reasons. Not that I needed further convincing not to jump, but that caution put some additional icing on the cake. The kids began to climb up the bank to the bridge, where the counselors would help them climb out to a girder from which they would jump. One after another, joyous, screaming kids would drop, hitting the water with a smack. A couple had stuck their arms out horizontally as if this would slow them down and grimaced as they later gazed upon their reddened arms. "Hit the water like a knife!" the counselors yelled out. My two friends and I watched the constant parade of jumpers, and when one of the counselors asked if we wanted to join in, he smiled and said, "That's fine," when we indicated no interest whatsoever.

After half an hour, we decided to climb up on the bridge and watch the show from above. That's when my heart sank as my friends talked each other into making the plunge. Each climbed out onto the girder and, after some coaxing from the group, went screaming into the depths below. I was now the ONLY one who had not jumped. The next few moments were a blur, and the next thing I knew, I was standing out on the girder. Had I lost my mind! To this day, I have no memory of climbing out there or what possessed me to do it, but there I was, looking down at the water 1000 feet below. I immediately decided that there was zero chance I would jump, and while I was going to be ridiculed for backing out of the jump, I was prepared for that. I was reaching back with both arms, securely holding on to parts of the railing, and all I had to do was turn to get back to safer ground. But turning would mean letting go with one hand and pivoting on one foot on a narrow girder. My terrible balance told me that this would be difficult at best. I was stuck! I imagined the helicopter dropping down a harness to get me off the girder. The kids were still yelling, "Jump! Jump! Jump!" However, their voices faded into the distance as I only heard my inner voices arguing over my limited options. Then for some unexplainable reason, I let go of the railing and dropped.

As the air rushed past me, I heard the warning, "Keep your legs closed," just as I hit the water. Before I knew it, I had surfaced to the cheers from above. What suddenly made me jump? To this day, I have no clue, but it had all transpired too fast to dissect. And then came the thought I would never have expected, "Wow! That was incredible!" Before I knew it, I had climbed back up on the bridge and again stood out on the girder. This time I let out the patented scream as I dropped to the water below. And then I jumped a third time, only stopping because it was time to load up and move on. In my mind, I had managed to do the impossible. The next day we did some more jumping from areas around Trenton Falls, and though I still wasn't comfortable looking down, I made the jumps.

I wish I could say I overcame my fear that day, but I am still terrified of heights. But more importantly, I met a monster that day face-to-face and did not back off. I've always heard that courage is not the absence of fear but facing that fear. We occasionally run into those monsters throughout our life, and while I still consider myself somewhat of a coward, I learned that day that I can tackle a monster if needed. It was an important day in my youth, a confidence build-er that was sorely needed. While heights still bother me, I under-stand that this is undoubtedly a positive for me. My poor balance and clumsiness would have resulted in a severe fall. I can get up when I have to, whether on a ladder or a low roof, but I am hanging on for dear life. I'll watch a roofer walking across a steep incline carrying a bundle of shingles and know that could never be me. I can live with that. Getting to know oneself means understanding physical limita-tions. Reasonable fear is a good safety net.

The incident also speaks volumes about that excellent camp where no one was forced to do anything. Hyde Bay Camp closed in 1969, but campers still return for reunions over fifty years later. The camp was a place where boys took significant steps to becoming men. Granted, sometimes youth need to be forced to take a big step, but when efforts come from within, it is much more meaningful than those induced by fear or an adult's command. I grew a lot that sum-mer, and that scared young boy began to put some of his fear in the rearview mirror. I often think of those few moments on the bridge and still wonder how I ever got the nerve to jump, but I am so thank-ful that in a rare moment, I just let go.

Where Have You Gone, Mr. Robinson?

It was the summer of 1954, and Memorial Stadium had just opened in Baltimore. My father and I had listened to a couple of the Baltimore Orioles baseball games on the radio, as we had no TV, and this Sunday afternoon, he was taking me to my first game. The stadium looked huge from the outside, and the hordes of people were intimidating to this five-year-old youngster. I remember holding my father's hand tightly lest I get separated in that ocean of humanity. We climbed up an endless ramp to get to the upper deck and soon walked through the concrete inner sanctum to get to the right exit. I had seen ball fields before but only with small bleachers, but I had no experience to prepare me for what I was about to see. We turned up the ramp, but I could see nothing because a crowd was in front of me. Suddenly the crowd parted, and my breath was taken away as I gazed out onto an immense sea of brilliant green. It looked too green to be grass, a giant painting, no doubt. This was a "Wizard of Oz" moment as color dominated my view.

The smell of peanuts and popcorn enhanced the effect. The Orioles were in batting practice, and although recognizable by their white uniforms, they seemed so small from this vantage point, two-legged ants scurrying as practice proceeded. The occasional crack from a bat hitting a ball reverberated in the park, and the field seemed endless. The Orioles were destroyed by the Cleveland Indians that day, with future Hall of Famer Larry Doby doing a lot of damage and another future Hall of Famer Early Wynn getting the win. Chuck Diering drove in the only Oriole's run that day, instantly becoming a hero, and the roar of the crowd was exhilarating. The lowly Orioles lost 12 − 1 and almost 100 games that year … but I didn't care! I was hooked, and baseball became an integral part of my soul.

Summers in Baltimore in the 1950s and 1960s would have been unbearable without Memorial Stadium and the Baltimore Orioles. Growing up just a few blocks from the stadium made the Orioles part of our neighborhood. We spent many afternoons at the stadium watching great baseball, and hot dogs and soda were like manna from heaven. The popcorn was much too salty, but who cared since it came in a conical container which soon became a megaphone. I'm convinced the excessive salt ensured one would buy a soda next. The evening games were an utterly different experience as the lights made the field glow, and no one ever mentioned a child's most hated word: bedtime. Living in a three-story row house in the city made sizzling summer evenings deadly, and a trip to the stadium was always a welcome escape. I can't tell you how often my father would jump up as dinner was nearing an end, exclaiming, "Let's go to an Orioles' game." My mother was never a sports fan, although she tried hard for my father. Someone needed to stay home with a younger sibling or two, and Mom was more than happy to wear those shoes.

Not only could we walk to the stadium, but the stadium was much more accessible than today. Fifty cents would get you a decent seat, and sometimes you could even get into the stadium free on an off day to watch a practice. The players would sometimes talk to you as they left the stadium after a game. I had a friend with a house right across the road from the stadium, and before the trees in the outfield grew up, we could sit on his porch roof and watch the game with binoculars. But nothing compared to the sights, sounds, and smells of the stadium, and the cheers of the crowd would send you scurrying back to your seat if you had gone down for food. Twenty-five cents would get you a soda or a tube of popcorn, and no game would be complete without getting something to eat.

Every child wanted to be the next baseball hero, and a nine-ty-five-degree summer afternoon would find the neighborhood kids all trying to prove they were the second coming of Babe Ruth. Mick-ey Mantle was the American League star in the 1950s, but he was a Yankee, a designation equivalent to being the ruler of the underworld. Ruth had also been a Yankee, but he was forgiven as he was from Bal-timore. While, sadly, our Oz was a predominantly white world, Jackie Robinson, Hank Aaron, and Willie Mays were our first connection to a more diverse world. Our exposure to those heroes was limited be-cause they all played in the National League with the Orioles in the American League. Joe Durham was the first black Baltimore Orioles player. When he hit a home run for the Orioles in 1954, even diehard Baltimore racists overlooked his race. It would be a long time before many would consider a black ballplayer an equal as a person, but to my friends and me, the only thing that mattered was how well they could play.

Two individuals had fostered my love of baseball, my father and my Uncle Teddy Hartman. While other sports may rival baseball in popularity, there is nothing that compares to the ritual of father and son playing catch. Dad worked hard to help pay for a house we could barely afford, but he always found time to play catch. He would ride the bus home from a long day at the office, and after changing clothes, he would pick up his glove and join me outside. Years later, I realized that after a long day, a parent wants to stretch out and relax, but Dad understood the paramount significance of the ritual. As the oldest of four, it would be a while before my brother, four years my junior, could master a glove. The game of catch with baseball and gloves is a primitive form of communication. No words need ever be spoken, but a bonding soon occurs. My father was not one to share his feelings or openly express how he felt, but the back-and-forth movement of a baseball between two people said it all. I was loved.

My Uncle Teddy Hartman often visited, grabbing a glove and joining me in the sideyard. I was the eldest of many cousins and three years older than the next male cousin. As did my father, he would often pick up a glove and join me for a game of catch. Unlike my father, who took the father-and-son catch as a serious ritual, Teddy was a first-class comedian. Jokes and physical comedy would happily punctuate the game of catch. As much as I enjoyed his antics, his attention to me at that stage of my life was profound.

My early Orioles hero was Gus Triandos, the Orioles catcher and home run leader. Our afternoons in Death Valley, our tiny neighborhood ball field, were spent trying to launch a home run as majestic as one of Triandos' moon shots. He hit 30 home runs in 1958 and was a three-time All-Star. That year he also caught knuckleballer Hoyt Wilhelm's no-hitter against the Yankees; 1958 was a fantastic year to be an Orioles fan. These accomplishments were more than enough to cement Triandos as a local hero. We ignored that he was a frequent out and that he may have been the slowest player in the league. On one hilarious occasion, he hit an inside-the-park home run against the Red Sox. As slow as Gus was, equally slow Ted Williams raced along the outfield fence trying to chase down the ball. The whole bizarre scenario seemed to play out in slow motion. No one knew whether to laugh or cheer when Triandos crossed the plate standing. Gus was my first sports hero.

At the end of the 1962 season, the Orioles traded my first hero, but this almost went unnoticed as Brooks Robinson, our third baseman, was emerging as the ultimate star. The incomparable number five became the heart and soul of the team. Brooks was my hero for many years, but then he was every Baltimore kid's idol. Number five wielded his magic on third base for two decades, making one impossible play after another. It was great that the world saw his unbelievable feats in the 1970 World Series. For two years, I played Little League baseball as a member of the Junior Orioles. The team had the correct name, and I was determined to play the position of my hero. While not having the glove, reflexes, or arm to play the "hot corner," I played third base for those two years.

If I had paid attention to several not-so-subtle clues, I would have figured out that I would not be following in the footsteps of the venerable Mr. Robinson. I had also played some youth lacrosse, and the coach actually came to our house one day to have my father talk me into dropping off the team. While that hurt, it energized me to devote more time to baseball. Our little league coach thankfully had a better attitude; he had to because he was stuck with twenty kids who were blessed with far more enthusiasm than ability. However, we set one Baltimore City youth sports record – thirty-nine consecutive losses. Our streak was broken on the last game of the second season as we played a team who had already won the division and basically mailed the game in. For us, it was winning the World Series. We didn't even know how to act when winning a game.

The first year, they awarded me a trophy, the only one I ever won as a kid. Before thinking I was talented, consider that the trophy was for being the best infielder on our team; thus, I was the best of four, three of whom could not catch a ball, and, thanks to my father, I could—most of the time. However, I didn't see any recruiters in the stands the following year. I remember that second year being booed by a parent after making an error. He kept calling for the coach to take me out of the game, and that's when I made the classic sports error—I began to overthink what was happening. Sure enough, when the next ball was headed my way, I was so stressed about making the play that the ball went right through my legs. My heckler now had company, and after a third inevitable error, I was yanked from the game. It was official now: I would not be the future Brooks Robinson. I opted out of the league's third year after things continued to spiral down. That second year did end on a positive note as I came off the bench to double, driving in two runs, in our only victory. But I treasured that trophy and kept it for years. It was the zenith of my athletic career.

I continued to play ball, but competitive sports were not my cup of tea. While I didn't play ball that third year, my baseball career was to have both its high and low points… at the exact same moment. On one ordinary day, our family went over to visit my cousins. With seven rambunctious children, the household was always delightfully chaotic. Several adults were in the living room, but to avoid copious introductions and dissertations on how big I was getting (even though I hadn't grown in the month since I'd last seen them), a cousin and I went out into the yard to play catch. In hindsight, I should have gone in to meet the adult visitors first because I was about to get the surprise of my young life.

After a few minutes of catch, one of the adults came out and asked if he could join us. He picked up a glove from the porch and strode over to us. What a treat to have an adult break away from the alcohol and adult chatter and want to associate with the kids; often, adults were simply happy to get us out of the way. I hadn't met the man before, but my cousin knew him. He fit right in with our game, but I soon noticed that he was quite adept with the glove. One of my throws went low and wide, and he quickly backhanded the errant throw on the bounce. Wow! This guy was better than my father. After a few minutes, my cousin asked me who my favorite player was. "Brooks Robinson," was a reflex answer. Another of my throws bounced in the dirt, and the gentleman quickly snatched it up. I was starting to be quite impressed. My cousin finally asked me, "Do you know who you're playing catch with?" I still was clueless. "That's Brooks Robinson!" I laughed, knowing my cousin was a classic joker, but I suddenly started matching the face with his picture on my baseball cards. It really was Brooks, who at this point was grinning from ear to ear. I was playing ball with my hero. He didn't look like an athlete, but then what is an athlete supposed to look like? He seemed an ordinary guy, but standing across from me was the greatest defensive third baseman who ever played the game. I couldn't believe this was happening. That's when, tragically, my brain kicked in again.

I wanted Brooks to see how good I was. After all, he was playing catch with the best infielder on the famous one and thirty-nine Junior Orioles. My cousin told Brooks that I also played third base, and Brooks grinned. A throw from my cousin got passed me, and after retrieving the ball, I decided to uncork an impressive throw to Brooks. The throw then sailed about twenty feet over his head. So much for impressing one's hero! As Brooks was a close friend and hunting partner of my Uncle Jack, I was to meet him on several occasions. He was even a better person than an athlete; modesty emanated from everything he said and did, and I was amazed that someone as good as he could enjoy poking fun at his rare miscues. If ever there was someone who could legitimately wield a big ego, it was he, but as I learned later in life, if one is genuinely good at something, bragging was unnecessary. I still use him as a standard for judging an athlete; consequently, few pass my test.

I have mixed feelings today about sports' importance in youth development. There is no question that it can be a positive factor if tempered with realism. Few will make it to the professional level, but teamwork, pushing oneself physically to a higher level, and learning how to deal with defeat are all positives. I was blessed with average physical ability but cursed with oversensitivity to the thoughts and reactions of others. Today we live in an era when we tell everyone that they are a star, admirable in one sense but quite unrealistic in another. Physical exercise is the real goal, and a certain level of competitiveness is a great motivator. I was lucky to have such a great athletic role model as a kid. While there was a greater chance of a hippo suddenly taking flight than my becoming a professional baseball player, a little dreaming is good for the soul. Brooks' natural athletic ability was a thing to behold, but his modesty is what I remember most. That professional modesty is so lacking today as money and stardom seem to be held higher than basic character. Brooks, thanks for the memories and for being the perfect role model.

The End of the World ...
Almost

Wednesday, October 24, 1962, was not a typical fall school day. Our family was usually talkative over breakfast, but this morning all were unusually silent, even my sister Gussie, never at a loss for words. Gussie would typically dip into her extensive repertoire of "Reasons Why I Shouldn't Have to Go to School," but today, she just fumbled with her breakfast. Dad's frequent recitation of news of the day was taking a break today, and Mom bustled around the kitchen fixing her standard breakfast. I'm sure I had a test or quiz that day as I was well into my eighth-grade year, but schoolwork was not on my mind. That week's news dominated all, and things had turned very dark the day before. After fighting and gagging through my mother's infamous oatmeal, I went into the hallway to get my bookbag. There was adequate time for the three-quarter-mile walk uphill to school, and I was in no hurry to get started, taking time to get down on the floor and play with our new beagle Dixie, already the fattest dog east of the Mississippi. The Cold War had reached a dangerous boiling point, and there was a distinct possibility war could break out that day. With the United States and the Soviet Union possessing a mountain of nuclear weapons, I could only think the worst, and for the first time in my life, I realized my home and family might not be here at the end of the day. I had watched the movie *On the Beach*, so I could vividly imagine how this would play out. My sister

Gussie started to sob and did not want to go to school. Her "Am I going to die, Mommy?" set my mother off. Next, Gussie launched into an impressive argument as to why she should not have to go to school since we would all be incinerated by the end of the day anyway. This just sent Mom to her bedroom in tears. Despite my attempts as the oldest child to be the strong one, I was choking on emotion and fighting back the tears. I walked out the door and started up the hill but turned to look at the house … one last time.

Welcome to the dark days of the Cold War when there was nothing cold about the escalating hostility. On this particular day, the Cuban Missile Crisis had reached a critical point as Soviet ships sailed toward an inevitable confrontation with President Kennedy's blockade around Cuba. I was born in 1949 when the Soviet Union unveiled and tested its first atomic bomb. While most children then were insulated from the events in the world, growing up in the shadow of Hiroshima and Nagasaki was unsettling, and fear of a nuclear war was the backdrop for much of the news then. Events had escalated throughout my first decade, highlighted by the Korean War (in which my father, now an Air Force Captain, considered getting involved), the anti-communist McCarthy Hearings, and the growing escalation of tensions between the once allied United States and the Soviet Union. In 1960, U-2 pilot Francis Gary Powers was shot down over the Soviet Union while doing a surveillance mission. Talk of a nuclear war became common, and no child was immune to this discussion.

Air raid drills were standard in the 1950s and early 1960s, and every school practiced response to these just as we have done with fire drills for years. Air raid sirens would go off periodically, and these deafening wails would arouse even the deceased. Years later, our two dogs learned to howl in perfect unison with the siren, and soon other dogs would join in, causing our entire neighborhood to erupt in one enormous siren that no one could sleep through. When the siren would go off, we did as Bert the Turtle said, "Duck and Cover"—duck to avoid flying debris and cover to prevent burns and falling objects. The standard response was to get under our desks and cover our heads; lucky Bert always carried his fallout shelter with him. By middle school, I was in a building with a basement, and I remember numerous times, upon hearing the siren, filing down into the basement where we crouched on the floor, covering our heads with our arms. While we enjoyed getting out of class, crouching on the basement floor was hardly a thrill.

Most didn't take fire drills too seriously since we obviously could smell no smoke and had figured that running away from a fire was no problem. But a nuclear attack was a different issue. All had seen film footage from Hiroshima showing buildings obliterated in waves. While having our school building reduced to a pile of dust was not an abhorrent thought for a young boy, being in it when that occurred was a different matter. I remember crouching in the basement listening for the sound of an incoming airplane, and it wasn't unusual to have a plane fly overhead during these drills, causing a significant visceral reaction in most of us. At these moments, I realized how ridiculous these exercises were. Being one floor down would not save our lives; even if it did, there would be no one to find us in the buried rubble. We had also been told that the radiation above ground would remain deadly for years so that we wouldn't survive anyway; better to be incinerated instantaneously. A child could tune out the news in those days, but the air raid drills brought it all home. Those could be terrifying moments for a child. Many kids made light of the exercises, but I had enough imagination and grasp of the news to respect them. My mother had a doctoral degree in worrying, and at least some of this had rubbed off on her offspring.

Since we were at home most of the time, every house was encouraged to build a fallout shelter. Plans were available for digging a shelter in your backyard, and numerous communities and neighborhoods did so. The fact that no one in our area had a backyard eliminated that as a possibility, but we had a good basement. I immediately convinced my father that we needed to build and equip a shelter in the basement. There were still windows on one side of the basement, but I figured the foot-thick walls would give us a fighting chance. Television, film clips, and magazines abounded with shelter designs, but despite all my warnings, Dad (wisely) could never find the time to build one. However, I was reading up on how to make ours and what supplies we needed to include. We had been told that even if the blast did not occur in the immediate vicinity, the fallout from the explosion could mean that we would be confined to a safe place in our home for months.

I decided it would be my job to save our family from the impending devastation. I identified an area in the basement, which seemed well protected on all sides, and set up some old chairs and a table that had been piled down there. Near our home, there was an army-navy surplus store where one could purchase anything from reconditioned work clothes to a hand grenade shell. After several days of pleading, I convinced my mother to take me there to load up on supplies.

The store had everything we would need to supply our air raid shelter, and my poor mother had to take things out of the shopping cart as fast as I could add them. Finally, we walked out of the store with three army-green blankets, six cans of emergency drinking water, some canned food rations, and a helmet, as if this would offer protection from a nuclear blast—my mother's attempt to humor her slightly paranoid and naïve son. And I'm sure those six cans of water would have gotten us through a year of living underground in our shelter. No one bought into my idea of a family air raid drill, and I remember being annoyed that most people just went about their lives, oblivious to our pending demise. I lay awake numerous nights wondering if the next day would be "The Day."

International events continued to deteriorate. In 1959, Fidel Castro had led a communist takeover of Cuba, just ninety miles from the US mainland, but that didn't impact me as these were just "gorilla rebels." While I knew they were human, my interpretation of "guerilla" meant a primitive force, incapable of attacking us. John F. Kennedy was elected President in late 1960, and he seemed to usher in a hopeful view of the future. He was young and dynamic and would indeed protect us. For a brief period, my fears of becoming a toasted marshmallow eased.

Sadly, this didn't last long. After Fidel Castro's takeover, Cuba became allied with the Soviet Union, and in April of 1961, the U.S. launched the completely botched Bay of Pigs invasion. With Cuba and the Soviet Union knowing of the attack in advance and multiple miscalculations and logistical errors, the maneuver ended up a complete failure, solidifying Castro's hold on Cuba and Soviet interest in the island nation. My fear resurfaced, and I returned to my plans for a family fallout shelter.

In October 1962, events significantly escalated as the United States discovered that the Soviet Union was erecting missiles on Cuba. One could rationalize that a missile from the Soviet Union would take enough time to get here that we would have time to react. However, a nuclear missile only ninety miles from the U.S. and directly south of the East Coast could get here with little advanced warning. I was terrified. One could assume that the Soviets were smart enough not to want to start a nuclear war, which would also obliterate their country in return, but twelve-year-old children are often more emotional than rational. We then learned that a fleet of Soviet ships, presumably carrying missiles, was headed to Cuba. In a bold and daring move, President Kennedy used U.S. ships to blockade Cuba, and a confrontation was imminent.

That led to the morning of October 24th. Heading to school that morning, I knew that the Soviet ships would encounter the blockade that day, and it was easy to see how the resulting confrontation could escalate into a nuclear war. Teachers treated that day as just another school day, and most students only wanted to discuss whether the Baltimore Colts would win their next football game. My thoughts were not on football that day and definitely not on math, history, and geography. I was often prone to daydreaming, leaving the classroom far behind, but this day, no spoken word ever made it up to my brain. I wanted reassurance from my teachers or at least news updates, but they wisely went on as if all were normal. Any external sound made me jump as I waited for the expected air raid sirens to go off. Thankfully, no one planned an air raid drill that day. This may have been the longest school day of my life as I kept glancing at the clock—wanting to see the exact time that the world ended. At least let me make it to lunch so I could enjoy one last meal!

When the bell finally rang at the end of the day, I sprinted three-quarters of a mile home. Racing into the house, I immediately wanted to know what was happening, but my mother, true to form, was watching her usual afternoon game shows and soap operas. While my father kept us abreast of news, Mom never wanted to hear any unwelcome news, and world news was often unpleasant. We could never discuss current events with her, and, with no twenty-four-hour news coverage as today, I would have to wait for Dad or the evening news. Once again, I listened for the air raid siren, hoping Dad would get home before it went off. If we were going into a fallout shelter for months, I wanted the whole family there together. At about 5:30, I heard the front door open, and I raced downstairs. The expression on my face must have given me away because Dad immediately told us that the Soviet ships had stopped short of the blockade, and Soviet Premier Nikita Khrushchev seemed willing to dismantle the missiles. For the second night in a row, I got no schoolwork done, this time joyfully planning the rest of my life, which could now take place. That event hardly ended the Cold War, but all could see for the first time that cooler heads would prevail.

A movie came out several years later, which should be mandatory viewing for all wanting to understand the irrational hysteria that often accompanied our reaction to the Cold War. What was missing from this earlier period was our understanding that the Soviet people were people with the same hopes and fears as Americans. *The Russians Are Coming! The Russians Are Coming!* came out in 1966, and, in marked contrast to earlier films, it portrayed the Russians in a positive light. The premise for the story is that a Russian submarine runs aground off of a New England island when the crew is trying to get a better look at the United States. The citizens of the tiny town overreact and panic, and the results are hysterical. The movie pokes fun at both sides but, more importantly, points out the ridiculous responses which irrational fear can provoke. The film was even shown in Russia to much acclaim and applause.

While there is no denying the seriousness of the Cold War and the Cuban Missile Crisis, the fear implanted in most American citizens did much to exacerbate the situation. Many were applying the domino theory to the spread of Communism—one country after another would fall like dominoes as Communism spread across the planet. This inaccurate and emotion-driven premise just fed and intensified the almost irrational fear that prevailed. We were just one generation removed from the war to end all wars … except it didn't! As a young child, I had not the life experience to put the whole tense situation in the proper perspective. Given unlimited resources, I would have built a bomb-proof citadel in our basement and stocked it with a lifetime supply of canned water, Spam, and Vienna Sausages (which my grandmother fed me on every visit—never had one since). In hindsight, I'm glad I was not shielded from the news, but clearly, I needed more background information to put it all in perspective. While the attack on Sept. 11, 2001, was terrifying for a younger generation, the constant specter of possible nuclear annihilation hung as a dark cloud over my childhood.

There is much debate about whether children should be exposed to the dark side of the news. With today's twenty-four-hour nonstop news coverage, compounded by social media postings, it is harder to insulate a child from significant news events. I don't see kids today obsessed with the negative side of life in the world, partially because they get desensitized quickly. My father provided rational commentary on the news I was privy to, and this allowed me to be aware with a proper perspective. However, so close to Hiroshima and Nagasaki, there was no covering up the complete devastation a nuclear attack would do. While sports, school, and family kept me focused otherwise, the days in the heart of the Cold War were terrifying ones; little imagination was required.

October 25, 1962, was a glorious day for that twelve-year-old child as my whole life lay in front of me—if I had only studied harder for the history quiz that day!

MR. RADCLIFFE,
YOUR DOG IS DEAD

The doorbell rang late one fall afternoon. Would this be the Jehovah's Witnesses again trying to help our family find salvation or another salesperson trying to sell us a set of steak knives guaranteed to be sharper than ... the knives they wanted to sell us the year before? We now lived in a large house in a pleasant neighborhood in northwest Baltimore, and we must have had a sign in the front yard saying, "Suckers Living Here—Will Buy Anything." No one in our household was making any effort to make it to the door, and when the bell rang a second time, I ran down to chase the peddler away. Dad beat me to the door, and upon opening the door, we noticed an older woman standing there, clearly not a salesperson. She was in tears; something was wrong. Had my brother been hit by a car? That had already happened once years earlier. It took her a while to compose herself, and she finally found the composure to say, "Mr. Radcliffe, do you own a beagle?"

My heart sank. "Yes, we do," Dad said, and I immediately started looking around for Dixie, then realized that I had let her out the door an hour earlier.

"I'm so sorry!" she said. I started to panic ... until she finished, "but your dog is dead. I don't think I hit it, but maybe I did. It's lying dead in the street. I tried to move it, but it was too heavy. I'm so sorry to bring you such sad news." Suddenly relieved, I broke into fits of laughter.

The poor woman was shocked at our apparent disregard for canine life. Lest she think I was completely insensitive, I now tried to explain, "No, it's OK. That's just Dixie."

"But she's dead; she's just lying motionless on the road. I shook her, and she's dead."

I continued to laugh, and the woman thought I was vying for the SPCA Monster of the Year Award. I told her to follow, and we walked out to the road. There Dixie was, lying in the middle of the road, completely motionless. The woman's car had stopped, but with the motor still running, in the street just short of Dixie's form. I called out, "Dixie, get out of the road!" She batted her tail twice, but her eyes remained closed. "I'm sorry, Ma'am, she likes to sleep in the middle of the road even though we try to discourage her. This has happened several times before. Thanks so much for caring to stop." After several unsuccessful attempts to rouse Dixie, I grabbed her by the collar and dragged her off the road onto the grass. She wagged her tail but continued dreaming of a land full of SLOW rabbits. She would have been named Lazarus if she hadn't come to us with a name already affixed. I thanked the woman, relieved and disgusted, and off she drove. Had she known the legend of Dixie, she would have understood. Seventeen years of beagledom made our rotund family pet as well-known as any dog in the city of Baltimore.

Growing up with beagles as pets is an adventure. So many of my wonderful childhood memories revolve around these silly canines with multiple personalities. But you have to understand—beagles are not dogs. They are a unique species. Dogs come when you call them; beagles don't. Euclidean geometry does not apply to beagles; for them, the shortest distance between two points is not a straight line. And a dog would never eat itself to death, but beagles? When we had a dog food scare several years ago, we wondered how much chicken, rice, and vegetables to feed our beagle, Maggie. The vet's assistant said to see how much she would eat in fifteen minutes and to use that as a guide. After she woofed an entire bowl down in forty-five seconds, we figured that she would have eaten her body weight long before fifteen minutes had elapsed.

As tragic as the loss of a dog is, the arrival of a new friend can quickly follow it. After Nickie's tragic death when I was twelve, our family wasted no time looking for a replacement. Once again, I picked out the first beagle we found. Dixie (already named) was the largest by far of a litter of beagles, and that should have given us a clue of things to come. This magnificent beast ruled our household for seventeen years, setting the bar high for any beagle to follow.

> **"We have a problem in our Roland Park neighborhood. Dogs are allowed to run wild, and there is one pack of dogs, in particular, causing major problems. The pack roams up and down the alley behind my house, knocking over garbage cans and spreading the garbage up and down the alley. I've had to pick it up repeatedly and have complained to the city, but the problem continues. The pack is led by a very fat beagle, who lets the others knock over the can, and then she pulls everything out of the can...."**
>
> *Baltimore Sun* Letter to the Editor, 1966

My dog was famous. Dixie was a legend in the city in so many ways. There has never been a dog quite like Dixie. Her exploits would fill a book. A fatter dog has never existed. At one point, she grew so fat that her stomach was getting raw from dragging through the grass. A diet, for reasons that will be obvious, was impossible; so Dixie often wore diapers to protect her belly. She ruled the neighborhood, and everyone knew it. She was at home in everyone's house, and we often had to call the neighbors to send her home. The neighbors also knew she liked to sleep on the road, and often I saw one of them dragging her off to the side.

She had no sense of smell from all that we could ascertain but would get up and charge off, as if after a rabbit, as soon as we walked out the door and then return to her usual sleeping pose when we went back inside. On one occasion on the family Spocott farm, she went off in pursuit of a rabbit. She chased it along the shoreline until the rabbit turned inland. For some reason, the rabbit suddenly stopped and turned to face the dog. Dixie screeched to a halt, continuing to howl. For some inexplicable reason, the rabbit started to hop toward Dixie. Dixie howled, went into reverse, and ran directly into the river, where she swam safely away, an amazing spectacle considering that beagles hate water.

Dixie was as round a beagle as there ever was, but it didn't slow her down or affect her exploits. One night I heard my mother and father stirring and turning lights on. "There's someone downstairs," I heard my father say. Not wanting to miss all the fun, I hurried down to the second floor with my baseball bat. Dad and I went to the head of the stairs, and we could hear movement from the dining room. As we crept slowly down the stairs, we could hear a rustling sound; my father called out to the "burglar," but there was no response. "Dad, it sounds like an animal has entered the dining room." Then I could see that the door to the powder room where Dixie slept was open. Uh oh! Dixie was on the loose. As we turned on the dining room light, there sat our beloved beagle… on top of the dining room table. She was chowing down on, of all things, a two-pound box of Swiss chocolates. Wrappers were everywhere, and as we got to the box, she hurriedly ingested the last piece. Chocolate, I had heard, was extremely harmful to a dog, and our eating machine had just devoured two pounds of rich chocolate, unwrapping each piece. Numerous times I have been told not to exaggerate so much. "A dog would die if it ate that much chocolate." But then, Dixie was no ordinary dog.

This was one of many gastronomic exploits undertaken by this legendary eater. My father had spent several years in the military during World War II and had, I'm sure, been exposed to some colorful language. However, to his credit, he demonstrated magnificent control in all my years growing up … except for one memorable evening! We were sitting out on the porch after dinner, talking and listening to the sounds of the neighborhood on a warm summer evening, when a blood-curdling scream rocked the silence in the house. Realizing it was my mom, we raced into the house and then into the living room. We all stopped in our tracks. There was this large black monster rolling around on the living room carpet. It bore a slight resemblance to Dixie, and we suddenly realized she was completely covered in something. Then we saw the large can we kept the bacon grease in. She was covered in grease and had been rolling all over the carpet to get it off. But this wasn't just any carpet; it was the pricey oriental carpet that my parents had inherited. That's when the only expletive that ever left my father's mouth thundered through the house. One thousand dollars later (and we were by no means wealthy), the damage was repaired. That's when Dixie acquired one of her many nicknames, 'auch gamitz," which Dad told us was German for "get out."

In her days in Baltimore with us, Dixie pilfered and consumed:

- A Thanksgiving turkey
- An entire ham
- Countless cookies and snacks
- And, in her proudest moment, in one sitting, fifty-four Little Tavern hamburgers which had been purchased for a neighborhood get-together. Guinness Book of World Records, anyone?

This did not include what she and her pack of dogs consumed from garbage cans. The larger dogs in her pack would knock over the cans, and the "leader of the pack" would climb into the can and begin to consume all edible contents. I don't know how often someone in the neighborhood went to right their garbage can only to find a rotund beagle inside. Despite this, she was beloved by most in the neighborhood. Her daily rounds would include visiting the butcher shop in the local grocery store, from which she would often return with bones as big as she was. My mother especially enjoyed it when Dixie would drag these greasy monstrosities into the house.

Dixie's size would have suggested a shorter life span, but she lived an active seventeen years. She came to rule our house for a large chunk of two decades. She was as delightful and friendly a dog as ever waddled the planet … with one exception. Woe is the person who would have the nerve to sit in HER chair. There was a red leather chair that sat for years in our living room in Baltimore. Anyone remembering that chair pictures a beagle spread out in it. During the second part of her life, she spent more than fifty percent of her time in this chair. It was the last place you would see her in the evening and the first in the morning. Occasionally some poor soul would sit in it, unaware of the chair's proper owner. My grandfather made this unfortunate error several times. Dixie would enter the room and approach the chair. The patented beagle stare followed this. "Hello, doggie, how are you today?" The look would continue. "Can I help you?" The stare would then turn into a teeth-baring growl. Not understanding the significance of the growl, my grandfather would end up with a beagle in his lap. A "get down, doggie" would result in another growl, followed by a beagle return to his lap. This sequence would continue until a victor was proclaimed, and Dixie never lost a confrontation. This was as gentle a dog as ever until one sat in her chair.

Dixie was one of my rocks during my turbulent teenage years. She was my beloved companion during those years when I struggled academically and socially. High school was not a happy time for me. While my parents were as loving as any parents could be, our home became dysfunctional. My sister Gussie's complex medical problems elicited several psychological responses, and my younger sister Kim, diagnosed as mentally retarded, was taken out of the home. The two monopolized my parents' time and attention, and I started a significant downslide myself. I became increasingly isolated socially, but I had a beagle, a tireless and devoted companion. Many days, Dixie and I disappeared for one of our patented "talks." She may not have understood my words but read my body language and emotion. I would get her patented lick at the right moment, and she certainly understood some of what was happening. I had the ultimate therapist, albeit with four legs. I survived these painful teenage years, but without Dixie, I suspect the outcome would have been far different. As Nickie had been several years earlier, Dixie was the source of so much joy and comfort. Leaving her when I went to college was difficult, but we always picked up right where we left off when I returned.

When Jackie and I married, we quickly acquired our own beagle, but there was always something special about returning home to my old friend. Dixie was now living at nearby Spocott, the family farm on the Eastern Shore, surrounded by rabbits who could not have been safer. She ruled the place as she had our home in Baltimore, and no visit to the farm was complete without a bit of time with her, a roll in the grass with her, and, of course, a long belly rub. Jackie and I had three children in a short interval, and they became our focus. When the fateful day came when Dad informed me that the old four-legged warrior had passed on, it was a sad day that elicited many memories. That blessed beast had saved my life in so many ways. I felt guilty for spending so little time with her those last couple of years, but to my father, she was royalty. Even my mother, never the dog lover, grieved. No dog lived a better life. As happy as I was with a wonderful wife, three children, and now two beagles of our own, a visit to Spocott now seemed empty. No longer did a rotund warrior come charging out to greet us and then go charging off to chase an imaginary rabbit, but the visits would unleash an avalanche of memories of growing up in Baltimore with my faithful companion. I miss her to this day because a little piece of me died with her. Every child should have a dog. I would say it is cheaper than therapy, but when I add up all that Dixie ate in her seventeen years, a therapist may have been less expensive. It is the unconditional love of a dog that not only comforts but teaches us much about what is good in life. Dixie rules heaven if dogs make it up there; it would not be heaven without them. She never caught a rabbit, but no dog ever ruled over those around her as she did. And if she brings as much joy in the great beyond as she did to me, heaven is a blessed place.

PYROMANIA FOR DUMMIES

There are many ways to measure intelligence. Some people have a photographic memory. Not only do I not have this ability, but I can forget a name in less than three seconds. If this is a sign that I have dementia, I developed this disease shortly after birth. My son Andy could quote back a short paragraph after reading it once. Four words are about my limit. He was once asked to leave a casino because he could count cards, yet this is the same person who called Jackie and me from town to find out what it was that we had sent him in after. My grandfather knew Franklin Roosevelt and marveled at his ability to remember a name. My father met Roosevelt when he was nine, and ten years later went to a White House social function, subbing for my grandfather, Senator Radcliffe. Not realizing my father was coming and having only met him briefly ten years earlier, Roosevelt wheeled over to him when he entered the banquet hall, saying, "George, it's great seeing you again." Without looking, I cannot tell you what color shirt I am wearing today. This is reason #134 why I could never be elected President.

Intelligence manifests itself in many ways, and I'm still looking for my manifestation. I would also flunk a spatial intelligence test, and I marvel at someone who can repair a car or disassemble something to fix it. Things I take apart stay disassembled. I am entropy personified, as I can quickly turn order into chaos. I might have a touch of musical intelligence, but the evidence is scanty at best. The fact that my teacher asked me to mouth the words for a school concert in sixth grade doesn't speak well for my having that ability. Artistically, I am a train wreck; let's say no more.

I recently found a doctor's report written while I was young, indicating that I might be below average in intelligence. I was shy and rarely spoke up in school; this might have contributed to my demeanor. If daydreaming is a sign of intelligence, then I must have been a genius because I was always somewhere else. I worked hard and got good grades, but thirty-eight years of teaching told me there was often no correlation between good grades and intelligence. In college, there was a guy in his sixth or seventh year of trying to complete the course of study who would, on rare occasions, even make it to a class. But genius suited him well. Once on a bet, he said that he could master ten languages in two months, and somehow, he managed to pull it off. After six years combined in high school and college, I still couldn't master French. "Parlez-vous français?" "Nyet!"

They say the apple doesn't fall far from the tree, but my apple must have rolled down a steep hill when it fell off my father's tree. Or, as they say, my elevator doesn't make it to the top floor, assuming I even have a top floor. I'll never forget that fateful day I decided to see if gasoline burns. Ok, so I knew it was flammable, but this is an eleven-year-old child we're talking about. Part of Baltimore had burned down in the great fire of 1904, and I was unwittingly about to attempt a re-enactment. Curiosity killed the cat and almost did in my father's son.

We had just gotten a gasoline-powered mower, a relative novelty in 1960. Now my lawn mowing resume was limited. In our first house, our yard had been so small that a power mower seemed overkill. We had a push mower that was a real workout for a young kid, but I could have cut the grass with scissors since our yard running alongside the house was no more than ten feet wide. I got proficient with the mower and made some cash by cutting the lawns of a few older women in the neighborhood. But when we moved to our second home in 1958, we had an actual yard to mow. My father got a gasoline-powered mower, but that was his baby. It cut through the thicker grass like butter, compared to the old human-powered contraption, which ran away when it saw tall grass.

However, this summer, I had been allowed to use the gasoline-powered mower occasionally. Dad had schooled me on safety and then turned me loose. On this particular day, Dad was out, and Mom was inside. She rarely came out and never did any lawn or garden work. I cut the side yard and, before moving out front, went back to fill the mover with gasoline. This is when curiosity almost killed the cat. I spilled a little gasoline on the ground. Even though I knew it would evaporate, I wanted to see it burn in front of my eyes, not concealed in an engine. I knew where some matches were in the basement and quickly retrieved them. No one could see me in the backyard as shrubs shielded us from neighboring yards. I lit the match and dropped it where the gasoline had spilled, but nothing happened. This is where my elevator cables broke, and my elevator dropped clear to the basement.

I needed more gasoline on the ground before it would ignite. I'd spill a little more and try to light it again. I then poured out what, in hindsight, was almost a quart of fuel, figuring this much would burn for sure. Before we continue this sad tale, let me share a few facts to show how brilliant this eleven-year-old was.

1. A quart of gasoline is enough to move a car up to eight miles.
2. My father never raked up his grass clippings, and a good layer covered the ground.
3. I left the mower and gasoline can within four feet of where I would drop the match.
4. I was ten feet from the house.
5. There was no water on this side of the house.

Considering none of these facts, this child prodigy dropped the match. When I regained consciousness in the Emergency Room .... no, that's fortunately not how it played out. I quickly discovered that a quart of gasoline would light immediately8 and that dried grass burns equally fast. What saved me was the fact that the wind was blowing away from the mower and gas can ... and house. Within a couple of seconds, the backyard was a river of flames, and the river was about to move up a short hill to the side yard, where there were cedar trees with all their needles. That's when this moron-in-training started doing his fire dance, madly trying to stomp out this large fire. I had seen how cedar could explode in a fireplace, and I now pictured the fire department soon trying to save our house as the cedar trees shot flames high into the sky. Citizens of Baltimore, bring on the marshmallows! My heart raced as I madly danced around. It finally occurred to me that water might help; fortunately, I knew where a long hose was. Five minutes later, all was thoroughly under control.

For the first time, I stopped to survey the crime scene. I had obliterated a 150-square-foot area of our yard. There would be no grass to cut here for quite a while as green had completely been replaced by black. Now the real panic set in: how was I going to get out of this mess? I had charred a sizable portion of the lawn. If I were lucky, the fire hadn't been noticed so far, and Dad would be out for another hour. Mom was asleep and wouldn't know what was happening behind the house. I immediately began raking and carting away all the charred grass clippings. However, a monstrous black blemish remained, and it would take considerable time before green would appear again. I began collecting grass clippings from the front yard and spread them carefully to cover the spot. I added a good quantity of "onion grass" to cover up the burnt odor, which still prevailed. It was a brilliant plan, as bright as my original plan to investigate the flammability of gasoline. I was finishing when I heard Dad's car entering the garage. He would walk right past this spot. That's when I looked down for the first time at my shoes.

I don't know whether the shoes had burned or melted or both. The white shoes were now black and molded into a different shape. I sat down and managed to get them off, throwing them into the bushes along with my socks.

Dad saw the mower and then looked down at my feet. "You really ought to wear shoes if you're going to cut grass."

I responded, "The grass is done; I'm just relaxing while I put things away. He walked into the house, and I breathed a sigh of relief.

But then maybe he had noticed. Dad had a way of putting me through psychological torture. Being a great lawyer, he'd leave you dangling until you finally hung yourself. There was a time several years later when a couple of friends and I had gone to Washington without telling him and Mom where we were going. We did nothing wrong; it was just a teenage escape. We got a hamburger and then drove straight back, but I decided to withhold the information for some reason. As we ate breakfast the following day, Dad, without even lifting his eyes above the paper, asked, "George, did you have a good time in Washington last night?" I mumbled a pathetic "yes," and that was the end. It was just his way of telling me that he knew.

I stewed for several days about being discovered, checking under the dried grass to see if there was any new growth. I wisely volunteered to cut the grass again the following few weekends. I never knew whether he had discovered the results of my failed experiment. There was no punishment that he could have doled out which could have been worse than the psychological torture I endured. Dostoyevsky would have marveled at my situation. I was lucky that day that an unpleasant situation didn't get worse. I wish Dad were here now so that I could assess his memory of those couple of days. He may have known, but ironically not punishing me was the worst punishment he could have inflicted. That day, I learned a lot: gasoline burns, and it is far less painful to "fess up." I ruined at least a week of my life worrying that a good gust of wind might uncover my dastardly deed. Clearing one's conscience is much less painful, but this is a hard lesson to learn. Confess and be done with it, and then life goes on. Unfortunately, this is a lesson many of us must learn the hard way. Dad also got his grass mowed for the remainder of the summer at no expense (not that he would have paid me anyway). He must have enjoyed that summer, watching me squirm while he just relaxed. Guilt is a powerful motivator.

Amazingly no one ever acknowledged my backyard barbecue, or at least Dad never let on that he knew how stupid his oldest son was. It was not a move that would get me an invitation to join Mensa anytime soon. Gasoline does burn! That day I completed the Stupidity 101 course, acing it with flying colors.

People sometimes consider me intelligent, but I remember the lawn fire and many other questionable childhood decisions. I've been able to function well in my job due to considerable effort. My wife Jackie thinks I'm intelligent, but she also thinks I'm handsome; her judgment is seriously impaired. In reality, we focus too much on intelligence. I've run into intellectual geniuses with no common sense whatsoever and individuals with so-called "average intelligence" who can solve problems with ease. Some individuals think of themselves as intelligent, but all one can see is their arrogance. Whenever one feels the urge to prove something, it usually is a cover for feelings of inadequacy. We can all contribute to improving the human condition, regardless of our intelligence level. I accept that I might not be the brightest bulb on the tree, but one reaches a point in life when the equipment we are issued feels comfortable. I don't aspire to be a Leonardo, Einstein, or Tchaikovsky. I'll keep on trucking through life, being the best me I can be. Several years ago, my granddaughter, Ellie, asked me to draw a horse, her favorite animal. I sent her, as I usually do, to have her grandmother do it, but at Ellie's insistence, I picked up a piece of chalk and started sketching on the chalkboard. She quickly erased my first and second efforts, but when she saw my third attempt, she immediately turned, calling out, "Grandma, can you draw me a horse?"

❖ ❖ ❖

"It takes something more than intelligence to act intelligently."
"When reason fails, the devil helps!"

- Fyodor Dostoyevsky, *Crime and Punishment*

Attack of the Troll

My parents entered their house after a delightful dance, a welcome escape from the trials and tribulations of raising their four active children. It was almost two in the morning, and the house seemed peaceful, a welcome change from the usual laughing and screaming that regularly shook the house. The babysitter was paid, thanked, and soon left with her boyfriend, who wasn't supposed to be there. As Dad saw the couple out the door, Mom headed upstairs to check on her children. Suddenly a scream was heard upstairs, "George, the children are gone!"

Racing upstairs, Dad started checking rooms. Kim and Gussie were not in their rooms, and a quick check of Bill's room found no one.

"Do you think they're all in George's room?"

"The sitter would have said something to us. Something's wrong."

Heading to the third floor, they checked my room, still finding no one. Mom was sobbing quietly at this point. All four of her children were gone!

❖ ❖ ❖

Eight hours earlier ...

My parents were hurrying to leave for the dance. Mom was upstairs, taking forever to get ready while Dad was dressed and patiently waiting downstairs, occasionally glancing at his watch. He was remarkably patient, but this scene was often repeated on the Radcliffe TV Network. I was downstairs entertaining Kim, my two-year-old sister, while Gussie, eight, and Bill, six, were playing upstairs in one of the bedrooms. Kim was still a couple of months away from being diagnosed as mentally retarded and had become quite difficult for my mother to deal with. Her development was regressing, and it was obvious to all that something was wrong. I'm sure Mom was looking forward to a stress-free evening. It was difficult getting babysitters for a family with four children, all of whom had a remarkable knack for attracting trouble. My father's job and status as a U.S. senator's son put him in the social limelight, and there was rarely a week when the two of them weren't heading out to a cocktail party, dance, or dinner. We dreaded these nights when we were young, but as we aged, we figured out what mice did when the "cat" was away. I remember one evening years earlier, chasing my parents' car down the road and hearing my mother say to my father, "Quick, George, hurry; he's gaining on us." We always knew when my mother was planning an escape because she would put on a lethal dose of Chanel #5, and this evening the aroma was particularly potent.

I thought I was responsible enough to babysit by the time I was ten, but my parents knew better. Our first-string babysitter was Mrs. Antonio, a much older Italian woman who constantly told us how wonderful her grandchildren were, implying that the four of us were not worthy to walk in their shadows. She did manage to make us behave, not an easy task, endearing her to my parents. We had two backup sitters, both neighborhood high school girls, whom we enjoyed, primarily because they would allow us to get away with anything, but this night none of the three were available. A new sitter was coming.

That evening Kim and I were running around downstairs playing a game. She and I got along famously, and she was my joy. My mother got the brunt of Kim's Olympic-caliber temper tantrums, while I usually saw Kim's calmer side. Kim was famous for escaping from the house and taking off down the street, and while Mom could never catch her, Gussie and I were able to track her down easily. Because of Kim's propensity for escaping, we knew my mother was particularly nervous about leaving her with a new sitter. Once again, I was given the job of feeding Kim, entertaining her, and then putting her to bed. Kim couldn't talk, but she and I had a nonverbal language that made supervising her relatively easy. The doorbell rang, and I left Kim in the living room to go open the door. I pulled open the massive door just as the caller was beginning to pound on the door and, for the first time, laid eyes on the Troll.

There stood Cruella De Ville, hair askew, chomping away on a giant wad of gum while smoking a cigarette. She had so much lipstick and make-up on that I thought this was a trick-or-treater arriving a couple of weeks too late. Still in high school, the Troll looked much older. The poor soul was almost as wide as she was tall, and with a voice that was a cross between a frog and an old man, she exclaimed, "I'm the sitter." Thinking that hiring this sitter must have been an act of desperation, I let her in the door. My father walked in and began giving her instructions just as Mom came down the stairs, telling my father what he had known for the last half hour, "We're late!" As they hurried out the door, Mom, in a moment of mental weariness, told the Troll that she could help herself to a snack in the refrigerator. Not to be disrespectful, but even the most casual glances at the Troll should have told her that this might not be the best idea.

The Troll did have a name, but I only remember her as the "Troll," a name Gussie bestowed on her almost immediately. She began laying down her rules, which consisted of these three edicts:

1. "Stay out of my way!"
2. "You all take care of the little kid."
3. "Where's the refrigerator?"

Gussie and I looked at each other, both knowing this could be a long evening. We decided that there needed to be a kids' meeting in Gussie's bedroom on the second floor, and we escorted Bill and Kim up there. We decided to give the Troll fake bedtimes to be able to stay up later, and I was to deliver this news since, as the eldest, I was the most likely to be believed. We decided to keep Kim away from the Troll, who looked like she could be dangerous. The smoke from her incessant smoking was already drifting up the staircase, spreading throughout the entire house. We could hear her downstairs in the kitchen, so I crept downstairs, leaving the others in the bedroom. Entering the kitchen, I could see that the Troll was already downing a coke and eating the largest ham sandwich I had ever seen. I told her all the bedtimes, to which she said, "You take care of them." At least that's what I think she said as half of a pig was rolling around in her mouth.

We had not had dinner, but we figured the safest strategy would be to stay upstairs the whole time. We could retrieve snacks from the kitchen as needed. It would have been a brilliant plan if only we had followed it. However, Gussie and Bill just had to look at the Troll again. After one trip downstairs, Gussie came racing back, boiling over with excitement. "Look, I found a picture of her boyfriend!" After Gussie explained that she had gone through the Troll's purse, I knew we were in trouble. We had to return it to her wallet somehow, but we were too late.

"Girl, give me my picture back!" the Troll shouted from the base of the staircase. We walked down the steps, not realizing what a mistake this was.

Gussie looked at the Troll and asked, "Who's your boyfriend?"

The Troll snapped, "Don't ever go in my purse, you ...."

Unphased, Gussie asked again, "Who's your boyfriend? I'll bet you love to kiss him." Gussie then began smooching the photo, making grotesque smacking sounds.

The Troll said, "That's Dick Clark." (Yes, the one and only, but we had no idea who that was at the time.) "Now give it back!"

Completely unintimidated, Gussie, in her inimitable style, continued kissing the photo, repeatedly saying, "Oh Dickie, I love you."

The Troll immediately took off after Gussie and the photo, with Gussie laughing every step of the way. We all followed her, wondering why Gussie was tempting fate. She was in no danger from the Troll, who was hardly built for speed. However, I wanted to get Kim out of a rapidly deteriorating situation. Our downstairs was a veritable maze, with its many interconnecting halls and utility rooms, making for several possible loops. The Troll started shouting and screaming, and for the first time, I grew scared. She next picked up a plastic baseball bat, screaming, "When I catch you brat, I'm going to beat you 'til you see stars." We raced from room to room, and as we went through the kitchen, I noticed several empty soda bottles and the entire ham now sitting out on the kitchen table. I got my two siblings safely upstairs and was returning downstairs when Gussie came streaking to the staircase, finally dropping the picture as she began to head upstairs. The Troll slowed down and picked up the picture. We needed to hide!

Soon we could hear the Troll downstairs talking to someone, but we could not pick up much of the conversation. It was too early for my parents to be home, so we crept out to the landing to listen. Hearing a male voice, Gussie whispered to us, "It's Dickie." Knowing the Troll was distracted, we decided that this was a suitable time to go down for a snack. If we were going to be stranded upstairs, we needed to have some emergency supplies. There was a back stairway leading down to the kitchen, and knowing that the Troll was in the living room, this seemed a safe move.

The four of us quietly snuck down the back stairs. We knew we were undetected as long as we could hear the voices in the living room. Keeping Kim quiet was a chore because she had no clue what was happening. Things were still in disarray from the earlier chase, chairs askew, trash can toppled, and numerous marks on the wall and floor where the Troll's bat had hit. There were six empty coke bottles in the kitchen, a once full loaf of bread was now half gone, and the ham had a substantial chunk removed. The Troll was going to eat us out of house and home. We had to stop her ... somehow.

Finding a box of cookies that would hold us over, we quietly retreated up the steps just as we heard the Troll and her company leaving the living room and heading toward the kitchen. Feeling that we had just dodged a bullet, we got to the top of the stairs and were high tailing it for the bedroom when we heard the Troll scream, "Where's my shoe?" Looking down, we suddenly noticed that Kim was carrying a shoe, obviously retrieved from the kitchen. "That brat's got my shoe now. I'll fix her." We were now racing for the bedroom as we heard her beginning to ascend the stairs.

Once inside Gussie's bedroom, we pushed the bureau in front of the door just as the Troll reached the doorway. She demanded we open the door and started to hit it with the baseball bat. This wasn't fun anymore, and we could feel her starting to push the door open as the bureau moved bit by bit. The barricade wasn't working, and we retreated into the adjacent bathroom. This door we could lock from the inside. We could hear that the Troll was inside the bedroom, and she was soon at the bathroom door. When she realized it was locked, she grew furious. She was crashing into the door, shouting all the while, and there was no doubt in our highly imaginative minds that she would hurt us if she ever caught us. I told her to just take the shoe when I realized Kim was still carrying it. The door would not hold out forever, and we were wondering where we could hide next when I suddenly realized that the bathroom had a door that opened onto a tiny porch. Once on the porch, we realized this wasn't any safer, but this porch was separated from the main staircase by a window.

The window opened about six feet above the stairs. After Gussie and I climbed through and lifted Bill and Kim down, we headed downstairs to plan our next move. We could still hear the banging and crashing up in the bedroom, and clearly, the Troll had not realized her prey had escaped. As we found out later, the Troll did not get through the door but broke one of the panels out. Furious, realizing she had been duped, the Troll headed out into the hall and began to head downstairs. The basement now seemed like a logical place to retreat since the Troll might not want to venture down into a dark and musty cellar. We left the lights off and carefully felt our way down the steps. Kim was starting to get scared and was crying a little. We comforted and continually talked to her as we made our way to the basement.

We lay waiting for the door to the basement to open, but there was no sound. The Troll, who had been cursing us, now grew silent. We sat on the basement floor, huddled together, and waited … and waited. Nothing happened. Possibly, she had tricked us and was down in the dark basement with us now. We were terrified and grew completely silent, listening for some evidence of her presence. We imagined her suddenly appearing, baseball bat in hand. Kim would suddenly move, and we would all jump. I could only imagine what a two-year-old was making of all of this. Finally, the waiting grew unbearable. There was no way to turn on the basement light because the switch was on the other side of the basement door. Gussie decided to sneak up the stairs and try to hit the switch. We heard her go up and then return with the lights still off. "The door's locked!" The Troll had locked us in the basement!

We waited for the longest time, but there was still no sound from above. The Troll was going to keep us locked down there. There was a door to the outside if we could only feel our way through the darkness. We only had our pajamas on, and there was no heat. Kim was cold, and Gussie and I hugged her to keep her warm. Bill was scared for the first time and started crying, while Gussie was amazing, fearless, and determined to defeat the Troll. She led us through the abyss to the door, and we soon escaped.

The frosty night air made us shiver, but after the darkness in the basement, it almost seemed like someone had turned on the lights outside. We thought about going to a particular neighbor's house, but alas, they had gone to the dance with my parents. We could call my parents, but the Troll had the phone number. The only solution was a return to the house to hide. We walked to the front door, but the Troll had locked it. We could hear her now talking in the kitchen. There was a porch off the dining room, but we would have to scale an eight-foot wall to get onto it. It was far removed from the kitchen, so this might work. Gussie was the climber in the family, and with a boost from me, she scaled the wall, stepping down onto the porch. I lifted Kim, and with me pushing and Gussie pulling, Kim made it onto the porch. It was more difficult getting Bill up, but he could pull himself up with help. I found a few cinder blocks to stand on, and with Gussie's assistance, I joined the group.

Fortunately, the porch door was open, and we entered the dark dining room. To get to the staircase, we would have to pass a doorway visible from the kitchen. If we could get past this point, I knew of an impregnable hiding place on the third floor. We heard the refrigerator opening and closing, so we knew she was still in there, feeding her face. Would the whole ham be gone at this point? We started to tip-toe through the room just as we heard her steps heading our way. We quickly dove under the table, making enough noise that we knew we would be caught. The dining room light went on, and she exclaimed, "I hear you. You're not getting away this time." Panic set in, and we crawled out and raced for the stairway. As I ran past her with Kim, I lost hold of her, and the Troll grabbed her. Gussie and Bill were upstairs in a flash, but Kim was in danger, now in the Troll's grasp. I turned to face her, telling her to let go of Kim. "I'll teach her a lesson. No one's going to take my shoe," the Troll responded.

Gussie had returned to see what had happened to Kim and me. We were terrified she would hurt Kim, who at this point was sobbing uncontrollably. Nothing we said made any difference. Our precious little sister was being held hostage. Then Gussie ran off in a moment of brilliance, returning shortly with the Troll's wallet from her purse.

"Give us Kim back, or I'll drop this in the toilet," Gussie shouted, turning and heading off into the house.

"You wouldn't dare. You little brat. I'll get you, too." But the Troll realized that Gussie was serious. She let go of Kim and took off after Gussie, who made a circle around the downstairs, ending up in the powder room.

Standing over the toilet, Gussie said, "Come any closer, and I'll drop it." The Troll had picked up the baseball bat again and was ready to swing away. With one swing, she smacked Gussie in the arm, and the wallet dropped into the toilet.

The Troll screamed and dove for the wallet, the threats now taking on a much more severe and vulgar tone. We were in real danger. As the Troll fished for her wallet in the toilet, Gussie, Kim, and I had time to escape. As we raced up the steps, the Troll was on our heels, swinging away with the bat. We heard the bat smack the floor and wall as she charged after us, cursing all the while. Bill was at the top of the stairs, and we grabbed him as we sailed by, moving quickly to the stairway to the third floor. The Troll was losing ground, clearly winded at this point. At the top of the stairs on the third floor was a large walk-in closet that could be locked. I knew I was tall enough to reach the key above the door, and as long as I could get the key and insert it quickly, we'd be OK. The Troll had just reached the stairway as we got to the closet. I dropped the key but retrieved it quickly. We were pushing the door closed just as she reached it, and as I heard the latch snap shut, I knew we were safe. There was a cedar closet inside this small room, and it had a light. The closet had several large wool blankets in it, and once the light was on, we were soon bedded down.

We were safe. The Troll was not getting in here, and we could wait it out until my parents returned. Kim was shaking but fell fast asleep once she was wrapped up in the blankets with us. I don't remember anything the others said; truthfully, we were too terrified and exhausted to say anything. Gussie, who was never at a loss for words, soon fell fast asleep, and I remember little after that until I was awoken by knocking on the door. I shuddered until I heard my father's voice on the other side.

As we emerged from the closet, it was obvious that the Troll was gone, and we were sent right to bed, a simple task since we were all half asleep. The following day, we surveyed the damage, and it was easy to see why Dad was so upset. The kitchen was a disaster, with every soda consumed and an entire loaf of bread gone. The ham was still sitting out with a significant section gone, the sink was overflowing with dishes, and we had to tell Dad that all we had was a box of cookies. The wood floors were scarred from the baseball bat, and there were marks on the walls going up the stairways. The smell of cigarette smoke still hung throughout the house, and the downstairs ashtrays were littered with cigarette butts. The cigarette burn on the dining room carpet upset him the most. We told him our story, and I'm not sure I would have believed what we told him if I hadn't lived it. My father remained very calm, and surprisingly there was no reprimanding us. He just excused us while he and Mom had a prolonged conversation. We never saw the Troll again, and interestingly enough, there was never any further mention of her. I have no idea how the issue was ever resolved.

I've often wondered what my parents must have thought and felt upon arriving home that night. To see all the devastation and then to realize that the children were all locked in a closet on the third floor must have thrown them for a loop. I can't imagine what story the Troll told them, and I never asked. While the memory now is a primarily humorous one, I realize how close we came to being participants in a horror story. And I'll bet my mother had a few words for the person who referred the Troll to her. But mostly, I remember a family of four children who bonded that crazy night, making the most of a nightmarish situation. We battled the mighty Troll and won. I'm all that remains of that band of warriors, and I miss them.

The following week Mrs. Antonio returned, and for the first time, we didn't mind her fussing at us and bragging about her grandchildren. Gussie was kind to her, which completely puzzled the woman. When she asked why we were so nice to her, I replied, "Oh, we're just happy to see you." I walked away with her still scratching her head in amazement. She let us stay up an extra half-hour that night. When my parents returned, the house was quiet, and they were delighted to find us asleep in our beds.

Living on a Pound of Butter

Growing up in a row house in Baltimore, I lived outdoors in the summer. My third-floor room was in the attic, and when the sun beat down on the roof, I could fry an egg on my desk. Houses weren't air-conditioned then, and only in later years did I get a fan. After breakfast, I ran outdoors, coming indoors only for meals. Since then, something about the outdoors has drawn me like a magnet. I'm hardly a candidate for an outdoor survival show, but it is still my continuing therapy. In my first few years, the outdoors was a place to play baseball in the spring and summer, build leaf forts and play football in the fall, and engage in epic snowball battles in the winter. At age eleven, I set off into the "wilderness" for my first big adventure.

That year I somehow talked my parents into something they should have never agreed to. A friend had grandparents who lived on a farm well outside the city, and he decided we should go camping there for a weekend. My mother was highly overprotective; I'm not sure why she agreed. She was stressed dealing with my sisters, and I'm sure I completely misrepresented what we had planned. Eleven-year-old children are remarkable in their ability to leave out enough facts from what they are describing that their story, while not a lie, bears little resemblance to reality. Rather than camping near the house, which I'm sure is what I told my mother, we were to be dropped off alone about a mile away in the woods. Off we went with a weekend supply of food and sleeping bags BUT no tent or camping experience and little idea of how to build a fire. We were city kids where the outdoors was streets, small lawns, roller skates, and bicycles.

My father often talked of his childhood scouting days, but because my mother was an indoor soul, he had never taken any of us camping. However, he suggested that I do a trial run in our yard. He showed me how to take a large tarp and make a simple A-frame tent open at both ends with stakes and string. I set it up in our backyard and was so impressed that when I looked in the mirror, I expected to see Daniel Boone looking back. No one else in the family wanted to join me for the backyard campout, so I was accompanied by my four-foot-tall bear, Chubby Tubby Timmy. The night went without incident, except I spent about fifty percent of the time going into the kitchen for snacks. I was ready, or so I thought, for the big adventure.

Frank and I were dropped off late Friday at a spot on his family's farm in Baltimore County. I had no backpack and borrowed a duffel bag my father had used in the military. Frank's family had packed the food, and he and I packed what we thought great outdoor explorers would need. This was going to be a simple exercise because we were … eleven with the innate wisdom of the ages. Have you ever tried to tell an eleven-year-old how to do anything? I rest my case. We started lugging our gear into the woods piece by piece, tripping and stumbling every step of the way. The great explorers had used pack animals, but my faithful beagle Nickie had remained home.

Once we had gotten far away from the road, we started looking for a camping spot. Near us was a slope with a beautiful stream flowing at the bottom and a ten-foot-wide shelf near the stream. This seemed perfect, and we started dragging the gear down the embankment. We could set up a shelter on the flat ground beside the stream. We had drinking water, but the stream would be great for bathing and keeping our food cool. What never occurred to us was that this narrow shelf of land had no vegetation and that there must be a reason for this. We were soon to find out why.

We used two trees as poles for our tent, and soon our tent stood erect. We then laid out our sleeping bags … right on the bare ground. We organized our gear and even suspended some perishable food items in plastic bags in the stream. The ghost of Daniel Boone was surely smiling down on us. We built a small fire, getting the sticks to light on only the twenty-second attempt with our next-to-the-last match, and we roasted hot dogs on sticks. We had, of course, brought along copious quantities of chips and cookies for a nutritionally balanced meal and stuffed ourselves until almost sick. In hindsight, this was a brilliant move. This was the life. We were masters of the universe, and I knew my dad would be applauding if he could only see us. We played around in the shallow stream until dark, deciding it was time to turn in. What we didn't do was look up and notice that the clouds were starting to build in the west.

We talked for a short while, and Frank fell asleep quickly. I lay there feeling quite proud of myself; I had had limited opportunity to be independent in my young life, and this evening was exhilarating. The night insects were awakening, and I heard a Great Horned Owl in the distance, the first I had ever heard. He hooted away as the breeze was beginning to pick up. "Hoo Hoo Hoo … Hoo … Hoo." The breeze felt incredible as I lay in a stuffy sleeping bag, which hadn't been aired out since my father had used it fifteen years prior. It never occurred to this outdoor genius that there might be a reason that the breeze was picking up after dark. The wind and wonderful outdoor sounds soon carried this intrepid explorer into the land of sleep and dreams.

I awoke suddenly as Frank was shaking me. Slowly gaining consciousness, I became aware of tapping on the tarp which covered us. Before the source of the tapping could register, I heard an impressive clap of thunder. I remember being thankful that we had put up a tarp. I had never been out in a thunderstorm before, but I figured we should be pretty safe at the bottom of a hill. The tapping increased in frequency, and soon we could tell that the rain was starting to intensify. And it rained and rained and rained.

The tarp was keeping us dry, but the rain just kept coming. We soon discovered that placing our tent right at the bottom of the hill might not have been the most brilliant move as water started coming in the side of our shelter closest to the hill. We quickly rearranged our gear to try to keep it dry. Being the geniuses we were, we had organized our equipment by taking it all out of the duffel bags and laying it on the ground. The rain continued to intensify, and our attempts to keep things dry grew more frantic. I was soon piling clothes on top of my sleeping bag and even stuffing some items in the bag. And it rained and rained and rained.

We quickly gave up trying to keep things dry as the water flowed like a stream through the shelter, and this was when we noticed that the water was also coming in from the direction of the stream. I aimed my flashlight out of the tent and noticed that the stream seemed closer than I had remembered. "Frank, was the stream this close to us before?" He was too busy rescuing his gear to listen or notice. I looked out again; the stream was beside the tent this time. Now I understood for the first time why there had been no vegetation on the shelf of land beside the stream. And it rained and rained and rained.

We abandoned our shelter within five minutes and moved part way up the hill. The stream itself now flowed right through our original shelter. We gave up all attempts to keep things dry; even our sleeping bags were drenched. The storm continued for what seemed like half the night before finally retreating to a steady drizzle. We sat on the side of the hill, completely soaked and clueless about our next move. The shelter was now sheltering the stream, and we were exhausted. I remember climbing back into the completely soaked sleeping bag and somehow falling into a state of partial sleep. That night lasted forever, as I'm sure the storm had stopped the Earth's rotation for a while. What had started as the hottest of nights now saw the two of us half-shivering in soggy sleeping bags on the side of a hill. How could one be cold on a hot night? I finally drifted off into unconsciousness.

As I slipped back into awareness, the sounds of birds told me that night had passed. I had ended up curled up at the bottom of a sleeping bag and began the progress of emerging from my cocoon. That's when I saw the devastation for the first time. Other than our suspended tarp, everything was gone. A large log was sleeping in our tent, and branches were strewn everywhere. The stream was back where it should have been, and we began the search for our missing gear. We did find the duffel bags and a couple of items of clothing, but pangs of hunger were going to delay the rest of the search. We had packed bacon and eggs to cook for breakfast, and a delicious meal would lift our spirits. That's when we noticed that the food container we had put in the stream was gone. The search became frantic as we realized the full extent of our plight. A long search turned up only a pound of butter which I had put in a bag in the stream but tied to a small log. Breakfast, lunch, and dinner were all gone.

The two of us discussed evacuation before finally deciding to bail out was admitting failure. Our chest thumping from the previous day was long gone at this point, but we were determined to get through the day. Pick-up was not until lunchtime the next day; we knew we could make it until then, and we still thought we could find the missing food downstream. It was a beautiful sunny day at this point, and we began hanging sleeping bags and any remaining clothing on branches to dry in the ever-warming morning breeze. We then started a systematic hunt for food, finally giving up after an hour-long search produced nothing. We returned to the campsite and retrieved our pound of butter. We each grabbed a stick of the good stuff, peeled down the paper, and began chomping away. We were going to make it.

For the rest of the day, we swam and explored, creating an imaginary land where we were now lords and masters. The day passed, the clothes dried, and we each had a second stick of butter for our dinner. We climbed into our sleeping bags only to find they were still quite damp, but at this point, nothing was going to keep sleep away. We had taken the tarp down and now laid on the hillside, using the tarp as a cover. We were soon fast asleep.

The following day, we began the lengthy process of hauling our gear up the hill to the roadside where we were to be picked up, a process simplified by the fact that much of our equipment was now gone. We had finally completed the move by 8:30, and our noon pick-up was a long way off. Frank suggested we walk to his grandmother's house, a mile away. We were dry by this point but probably quite a sight. What a brilliant move that turned out to be as his delightful grandmother fixed us a meal fit for a king. We decided this wasn't "cheating" since we had made it through both nights. We ate a mountain of eggs and a pound of bacon, to then be greeted by a monstrous stack of pancakes. We ate and ate and ate, barely making it back to the pick-up spot in time. Neither of us said a word about the incredible breakfast, and Frank's grandmother vowed to keep it a secret.

My parents had been aware of the Friday night storm and were glad to hear that all was well. Thinking that we were camping right beside a house, they must have assumed we went in under cover during the storm. We assured them that our "tent" had withstood the deluge and that we had come through unscathed. A year would pass before I would go camping again, but I had learned some valuable lessons. This city kid had learned a lot the hard way, and memories of all the discomfort soon faded away. I was hooked on the outdoors and would spend many more nights under the stars in the years ahead. I always planned for any eventuality, and even though I've encountered many storms over the years, I never sank as low as I did that one night.

There is something magical and primal about spending a night under the stars. It approaches a religious experience as one sheds the comforts of modern life to commune with the elements: the smell and crackling of an open fire, the call of an owl, and the comfort and security of a good tent and sleeping bag on a frosty night. No home-cooked meal ever compared to a breakfast cooked over an open fire, but I learned on that memorable trip that man does not live by butter alone.

CHILDHOOD MONSTERS

I never enjoyed English class: grammar, often reading literature that put me to sleep, never being able to get an "A" on any essay, no matter how much time I put in. This particular day, however, was one I especially dreaded. Our class was reviewing homework I had done with little trouble, and the teacher was going down the rows and having each person answer a question, all multiple choice. Whoever created multiple-choice grammar exercises missed the instructional lesson on engaging students in learning enthusiastically. I knew the grammar rules being drilled, but did we need fifty practice questions? However, today fear replaced boredom. I had taken the time to calculate that I would answer the twenty-third question, a question I had quickly answered. When the teacher got to me, I simply had to say "d," the correct answer for that question. So why was I terrified? I had to say "d," but I was a stutterer, and there was no way a "d" would emerge from my vocal cords, that or any day. I tuned out the class as I mulled over the three possible ways of dealing with this middle school crisis: give the wrong answer as "a" and "c" were simple to say, try to force out a "d," which would have meant stammering and sputtering repeatedly, or say "I didn't do my homework." I grew increasingly nervous as the questioning got closer and closer, and I started sweating profusely. Finally,

"All right, George, answer number twenty-three."

Silence as I tried to force out a "d," using every bit of energy in me.

"Uh, George, just give us the answer you have."

More silence as I realized no "d" was coming forth.

"Well, George obviously didn't do his homework. John, you answer number twenty-three."

The class snickered, and I could tell the teacher was angry. This had happened before, and it would play out many times again. I grew to hate school and would spend the day dreading being asked a question rather than paying attention to the content. In fifth and sixth grades, I had consistently been near the top of the class. By eighth grade, I was sinking fast; by senior year, I was ranked forty-eight out of sixty-four in my class.

❖   ❖   ❖

Children often create their monsters, and stuttering was my fire-breathing dragon. While there may have been some physiological basis for my problem, I elevated it to a significant problem in my mind. Years later, I still qualify as a minor stutterer and can see the humor in my earlier plight. However, when I was young, there was no humor to be found.

Those around me should have noticed the gradual decline beginning in seventh grade; if my parents did see it, they never discussed it with me. They knew all was not right with me, but then they were preoccupied with my two sisters, who had much more severe problems. My little sister Kim was mentally disabled and left our home at four. At the same time, Gussie's major medical issues were manifested in severe behavioral problems even before she hit her teen years. These coincided perfectly with the emergence of my stuttering.

I don't know when I first noticed that I stuttered. My parents told me I was taken to a speech specialist when young, but I have no memory of this. My mother was told that whatever problem I had was due to her not letting me cross the street. She allowed me eventually to cross the road, which had no recuperative effect. This is a typical example of how we try to find one cause for something when, in fact, most complex phenomena have multiple and complex caus-es. I was shy, and this helped conceal whatever problems I had. By the age of twelve, I was aware that I stuttered. Had I just never paid any attention to it previously, or did becoming more introspective at that period focus my attention on what was then a minor speech impediment? Some stutterers stammer through a speech blockage until they finally get their thought out. I took the coward's approach: don't speak.

My issue was just with the initial sound. If I could get the first word out, the rest always followed. However, the more I thought about what I was to say, the less chance there was of anything coming out. Certain consonants ("d," "k," "t") gave me problems, but the more nervous I got, the less chance I could say anything. I was considered shy by all, and none knew the real cause of my shyness: you can't look stupid if you keep your mouth shut. Surprisingly, I liked public speaking because I could script a talk that avoided all the words that would trip me up.

I went from absolutely loving school to dreading most aspects of it. I would do anything to get out of it, and having a radiator beside my bed meant I could develop an instant fever whenever I needed a good excuse to stay home. Middle and high school became an ordeal, and I began to withdraw from the academic side of life altogether. Once an avid reader, my free time was now devoted to worrying and doing anything to escape the worry. French class was a nightmare; those French pronunciations were not rolling out of my mouth. At home, things were fine unless … the dreaded telephone rang. "Hello" could never quite make it out of my vocal cords. I acquired a doctor-al degree in telephone avoidance. When it rang, I always ran as far away from the phone as possible. When I heard, "George, would you answer the phone," I had a remarkable litany of excuses. I don't know whether my parents caught on; they must have thought I was just the typical lazy teenager. When I did have to answer, the caller was often greeted by silence on the other end. I started getting creative, sometimes doing a great impression of a bad phone connection. This gave me enough momentum to finally utter something like, "What's wrong with this crazy phone?" My stuttering ensured that I wouldn't date much because I would have to call and certainly couldn't date a Debbie or Dorothy.

I look back on these days now with a sense of humor, but to this day, I can see how my education suffered. I no longer considered myself intelligent and fell far enough behind that catching up was difficult even if I could focus. We all suffered through those teenage years, and my suffering was self-imposed. I look back in amazement that no one noticed that I was self-destructing. My loving parents were suffering as my sister started running away from home, and my teachers surely should have noticed. I even got up the nerve in ninth grade to speak to my French teacher, who just ignored me, suggesting I would do better if I studied harder. While he was right, he ultimately failed to see what I was trying to tell him. The surprising thing is that I somehow got into a good college. I continued the downhill spiral in college until I had the nerve to accept a blind date for a weekend … with my future wife, Jackie. It's funny that "j" sounds were ones I often had difficulty saying, but the word "Jackie" rolled out of my mouth easily.

Ironically, I still stutter; I learned to hide it so well that few are aware of it. After several years, I subconsciously learned never to begin sentences with specific sounds or could recover immediately with a different word if the first one failed me. Stuttering was my "monster," and I finally slaughtered it. My mistake was never sharing my monster with others. I don't remember conversing with my parents about it all those years. Demons that one hides from grow in size.

As a child, one feels like they are the only one with a problem.

Later we find that we all had our own "monster": an abusive or alcoholic parent, a physical problem, poor athletic ability, a learning disability, or just the usual social nightmares and hurdles we all encounter. And then there were all those people suffering from discrimination who never had the opportunities afforded me. How nice it would be to have that perspective when young or to be able to have the humorous outlook we have later in life. My problem was so insignificant compared to many I knew: a classmate who died of leukemia at age thirteen or one that saw both parents die in an airplane crash while landing. How silly my stuttering was; I created the monster myself and fed its growth for years.

There may have been some physiological basis to my stuttering; I'll never know, nor does it matter at this point. I have to believe that my monster was primarily created within myself. My sister, Gussie, on the other hand, had a real monster. She was born with a circulatory defect in her hip that crippled her. As a child, I was aware of a massive congenital scar, but only later did any of us realize the pain she was in. As a doctor later shared, every step Gussie took in her life would have felt like someone sticking a knife into her joint. In hindsight, I feel foolish for focusing on my problem. But then, as children, we are self-absorbed, and it is hard to climb out of our shells to understand what someone else is going through.

But these real, created, or imagined monsters can serve a useful purpose. They toughen us for life's numerous pitfalls. Even though I had a relatively easy and pampered existence growing up in Oz, my monster prepared me for life as an adult. If you can slay a monster as a child or adolescent, the many adult monsters we face seem surmountable. The problem is that one must get past assuming that people won't understand or that our situation is unique.

I grew up in an upper-middle-class home surrounded by caring people. There was always a meal on the table, and we felt safe. While the issues with my sisters imposed a severe financial strain on our family, I was insulated from any economic problems. Santa was always generous to me, my grandfather paid the way for me to get into an excellent private school, and I always felt the love of two wonderful parents – hardly the prerequisites for a person deserving sympathy.

My stuttering monster toughened me more than anything else in my childhood. I am still a stutterer and, ironically, better off because of it. I have been blessed overall with a wonderful life, and I accept my monster as just a tiny part of who I am. Ironically, I chose to teach, knowing that my monster lurked beneath the surface, but it was the perfect choice for me. And while I can laugh at my stuttering and the torture I endured, fifty years later, I still cringe when the phone rings. Please email or text me!

Sunday Morning Milkshakes

Sunday mornings for this teenage boy were challenging, but then so were Mondays. Tuesdays, Wednesdays, Thursdays, Fridays, and Saturdays. Monday through Friday were school mornings where I had to get up early to do the homework, which I did not do the night before, and Saturday morning began with the ritual weekly chores. Several times each year, my father would decide we all needed to switch rooms, and the whole family would roll up their sleeves those Saturdays for a day of carrying furniture up and downstairs. Other Saturdays would begin with mowing grass, raking leaves, or cleaning our bedrooms, which managed to self-destruct without any apparent effort. Sunday, however, was my day, or so I thought and eternally wished for. That day began with the bane of my existence, church, followed by an hour or more in Sunday School, watching time go in reverse as the class discussed the "mystery of faith;" the only mystery to me was why, if this was all so important to the Big Guy, he didn't beam it down to us while we were sleeping. Getting to church, however, was anything but boring, and in our family, often elevated to an Olympic event.

Church began at 9 AM, or at least that was what we were told, but since we were never there to see the service begin, we only assumed that was the case. My mother had carefully calculated a plan to let all sleep until the last possible moment. She had given up getting the family up early because my sister Gussie would always take ten minutes more than the allotted dressing time, whether a half hour or two hours. This particular morning, the first call to get up came at 8:20; that meant we could lie in bed until 8:30. My mother would need this time to sort through her 125 pairs of shoes (no exaggeration … I counted) to see which would match the dress she was wearing. She had breakfast down to a science; if the military were only that efficient. Knowing that it would take fifteen minutes to drive to the church and another five to park and find our way in, coming down to breakfast at 8:45 left a negative five minutes for the meal. Still, Mom insisted that breakfast was the day's most important meal, warranting a balanced meal every morning.

To make matters worse, the Catholic Church had thrown in a wrinkle, part of the papal plan to make us suffer as much as possible since suffering was supposed to be good for the soul—I never bought that line. Suffering was supposed to make us more receptive to the "mystery of faith," but I had problems with a deity who thought suffering was a positive experience. To receive communion, one had to fast for three hours before taking communion. This was a vast improvement over the previous fasting from midnight on. Going to an 11:30 AM mass on an empty stomach was not a positive experience for a young child, and one could hardly follow the service over the grumbling of one's stomach. Fasting for three hours barely qualified as "suffering," but for a 9 AM mass, this meant getting up at 6 AM for breakfast, which wasn't going to happen. However, one could drink up to one hour before communion, reducing the number of dehydrated parishioners passing out in the pews. This gave my mother the ultimate solution to the whole breakfast issue, one that would require a blender—liquefy breakfast.

Mom had calculated that since communion usually occurred forty minutes into the service, we could drink up to twenty minutes before the service began. She simply would turn our breakfast into a "milkshake." This wasn't just an ordinary shake; it met all the minimum daily requirements. After the milk and a scoop of ice cream, she added eggs, bread, sausage, and who knows what else. I always wondered why there were no leftovers in the refrigerator. I, of course, was never up early enough to see what went in. I would ask her whether "blending" a solid turned it into a liquid. Weren't bread crumbs still solid, just in minute pieces? This argument did not sit well with a frustrated woman trying to herd her sloth-like offspring out the door. "Your brother would be happy to drink yours if you have a problem." Throwing chemistry aside, I would pick up my wonder shake with Mom shouting all the while, "only 45 seconds left to drink it."

This Sunday was Easter, and things were off to a particularly bad start. I was ready on time as I had not bothered even to clean up or brush my teeth. Gussie couldn't find the dress she wanted to wear, but then she hated wearing any dress. Bill had gone out to feed his turtles, which resided in our window well, somehow managing to come in covered with mud. Mom ordered him to change, and he returned wearing the dirty clothes from the day before. They were handed their milkshakes as they passed out the door while arguing with what was now a thoroughly frustrated and exhausted mother.

We arrived at the Cathedral of Mary Our Queen in Baltimore well after the service had started. You know you're late when you arrive at a church that can hold 2,000 people, and not a single person is anywhere to be seen outside. Finding a seat on Easter was always an issue as all the "Easter Bunnies" were out in full force, showing off their latest spring fashion. Mom always had to park in her favorite spot, allowing us the quickest getaway possible after the service. She calculated this without the help of any computer program and had it down to a science. We would save ninety seconds of getting stuck in traffic after the service, but it would take an extra ninety seconds to walk to the car. This meant we would access the church from the front, entering right beside the communion rail. Despite her children's pleas to enter from the back, Mom would do this her way. To add to the horror of the situation, the service that day had progressed to the point where the priest was well into his sermon. Two thousand people would be looking right in the direction of where we were entering!

Gussie and I figured we could enter and go down the side aisle, hiding behind the massive pillars as we raced in spurts down the aisle, but Mom had other plans. She was going to walk right across the communion rail, underneath the pulpit, and then turn to walk down the center aisle of the church past all 2,000 people. Panic set in, and I seriously contemplated turning around and running as fast as I could from the church, but my mind went blank, and this sheep blindly followed the shepherd. Wishing I possessed an invisibility cloak, I held my breath and all but closed my eyes. I was already the fifty-ninth most popular person in a class of sixty, and that final spot now had my name on it. That's when a terrible situation turned horrific.

As we were halfway across the communion rail and directly under the pulpit, Mom, turning around to urge on her terrified children, stepped into a heating grate, getting her high-heeled shoe stuck in one of the holes in the grate. Without losing a step, she stepped out of the shoe, removed the other shoe, and turned to me, saying, "George, get the shoe." She and my siblings took off down the aisle.

I bent down to get the shoe, which would not budge. Dazed, I had forgotten about the service and sermon until I heard the priest stop and say, "Having trouble down there, sonny?" Snickering and laughter started to spread through the assembled masses as people who had seen me suddenly duck down wondered what was up. I tugged and tugged, but the shoe was thoughtfully implanted. The priest had stopped the sermon and was gazing down at me while people in the front few rows peered down to see what I was doing. Should I leave the shoe and run? Maybe, just busting off the heel was the best plan, but then my mother would have two seriously mismatched shoes. I struggled for an eternity until the shoe finally broke loose. As I stood up, I was reminded once again of how many people were in that church because every one of them was staring directly at me. Then I began the longest walk of my life. I've hiked small sections of the Appalachian Trail, but nothing equaled the 100 yards I walked that day carrying the red high-heeled shoe. How would I ever explain this to my friends? A daring rescue of a small child or helping an older person off the floor would have helped my reputation, but how does one explain carrying a high-heeled red shoe through the church?

Additionally, I had to find my family in a sea of smiling and laughing faces. I had marched most of the way toward the back of the church and was seriously considering just continuing out the back door when my sister signaled me from the next to last pew, a few short feet from the back door, from which we could have entered completely unnoticed. And there were no grates back there! The sermon had resumed by this point, but all I could remember was the sea of faces staring at me.

I would never be able to show my face again anywhere within 500 miles of this point. This was as bad as the time I had bent over, ripping my pants at a service dedicating this same church a year earlier ... and that had been caught on TV, prompting the temporary nickname of "Moonman." If the Catholic Church thought that suffering made one more receptive to the "mysteries of faith," then all churches should have grates for floors, and high-heeled shoes should be mandatory. That Sunday, life was changed forever (or at least it seemed that way). Mom didn't even say "thanks" when I reached the pew because she was busy belting out a hymn.

Time eases all pain, and before long, I was focused on the next "most embarrassing thing I ever did." I remember bringing up the incident many years later, and no one remembered it. Like so much in life, the incident just became one of the things which toughen us in the painful transition from childhood to adulthood. It only brings a smile to my face now when I think back to that long march up the center aisle. My mother never succeeded in her quest to make me a good Catholic son, and organized religion, or my lack thereof, became a sore point in our relationship for years until dementia sadly wiped her memory clean of all that had happened. My resentment that day quickly disappeared as I realized that as different as Mom and I were, we both had the essential things in common ... love, family, and respect for others. I'm sure I embarrassed my children on many occasions. Looking back on that year in our lives, I realize the emotional turmoil my mother was experiencing with having to institutionalize one of her daughters and seeing another beginning to have serious personal issues. Children imagine their problems to be monsters when, in fact, they are dwarfed by what parents must surmount daily.

I once thought of my mother as a weak individual, but with time I've realized that the weakness at the time dwelled in me. She surmounted obstacle after obstacle in her way and lived life on her terms. Sadly, she outlived three of her four children but still maintained a positive outlook on life. The stubbornness and determination I saw in her are now an established part of me. My mother's knowledge of science may have been lacking, and I'm not sure what the Catholic Church's policy is regarding the consumption of suspensions before communion. I still wonder what she snuck into those chemical conglomerations. While I haven't had one of those "milkshakes" in over fifty years, they were a creative solution to a problem.

The Death of a
Thirteen-Year-Old

We all have incidents in our life that mark us significantly. Whether good or bad, certain moments define us as individuals. One particular afternoon in eighth grade devastated me and partly diminished any growth I had made that year. To this day, it is probably the most embarrassing moment I have ever encountered, and it certainly contributed to a downhill spiral that laid waste to much of my high school years. A teacher's insensitivity devastated me that afternoon and ironically led to my being a slightly different kind of teacher in later years.

Grade eight had been an uneventful year. A couple of years earlier, our family had moved to a different neighborhood within walking distance of the school. Home life was more unsettled with the issues my sisters were facing. Puberty was still well down the road, but I was still growing at a brisk rate. Each school day was long, with the day ending at 5:10 PM. Mid-afternoon, we had a long athletic period, followed by over an hour of study hall, still not enough time to complete the daily homework.

On this particular day, all the eighth graders were in one large room for study hall with Mr. Smith in charge. He was an intelligent man and dedicated to the school and his job, but if he had a human side, he rarely showed it. He used intimidation to help discipline, but I was a good kid, where intimidation did far more harm than good.

I avoided him like the plague, and while he never mistreated me, I remember nothing positive ever emanating toward me. I was not a favorite, but then, as shy as I was, I was no one's favorite. I liked my classmates, but as we were all maturing, I was starting to feel increasingly like I had been dealt a bad hand. In other words, I was an average thirteen-year-old boy.

I tried to concentrate on a math assignment that afternoon. Math was a breeze for me, so I always got it out of the way first. It was about 4:15, and as my body unwound from the physical exertion from earlier athletics, my bladder started telling me it was full. I had been slow getting a shower earlier and had raced back to study hall lest I have to deal with an angry Mr. Smith. I was kicking myself for not leaving enough time to hit the bathroom, and now I realized that I might not make it the hour or so before dismissal. I kept going back to the math to take my mind off the building physiological pressure, but my bladder was overriding my brain at this point. Mr. Smith had just announced that no one else was going to the bathroom as a part of a speech about how intelligent boys thought to use the bathroom before study hall. I was never going to make it.

The seconds became minutes, and the minute hand was frozen. 4:20, and I had fifty minutes to go. I dug into my vast repertoire of strategies for keeping the bladder full. I started running in place while sitting in the chair. I squirmed from one position to another, hoping to find one position that would diminish the ever-growing need. 4:25, and I was losing my mental willpower. I raised my hand, but Mr. Smith was busy grading papers and did not notice me. I cleared my throat, but the sound was lost in the large hall. A friend in front of me turned around and smiled as he realized my futile attempts to rouse Mr. Smith. Near desperation, I finally jumped up, and half raced to the front of the room. Mr. Smith saw me coming, and although I was trying to indicate I had to go, he sternly motioned for me to return to my seat.

The short walk, although futile, did calm my bladder temporarily. But not for long! 4:35, I was ready to burst again. In hindsight, I should have just run out of the room, but I was a shy kid and knew Mr. Smith's propensity for embarrassing disruptive students. His favorite strategy was having them stand against the wall, holding an eraser between one's nose and the wall. If the eraser fell, one would have to serve detention or Saturday school. Many students underwent extraordinary body contortions to keep that eraser from reaching the ground. The sight was always a blast for the spectators but pure misery for the victim. I was not going to become the class laughing stock that afternoon, but that would have been heaven compared to the path I finally chose.

4:40, and there was no way I would make it another thirty minutes. At this point, I was running four-minute miles in my seat, and anyone looking at my face would have thought I was about to give birth. I was in agony, and any thought of doing any work was long past. I was in desperate mode, and my brain was racing for some solution. We eventually reach a point where the body can no longer hang on, like a drowning person avoiding making that fatal inhalation of water. Finally, as they say, the floodgates opened! And did they ever open.

There was no stopping the flood once it started, and I quickly tried to think of what to do to cover the disaster. There was now a significant puddle under my desk, not to mention what my pants now looked and felt like. The second or two of physiological relief quickly dissolved into panic. The classmate in front of me turned around and looked under my desk. "Somebody must have spilled some water," I quickly said. I knew immediately that this ranked among the most ridiculous comments ever made. Water just miraculously appeared under a desk, and it smelled like urine. Right! Invisibility sounded like a workable solution, but I could hide neither the puddle nor myself. That was the longest thirty minutes I ever suffered through. The bell rang at 5:10, and the class quickly filed out of the room, leaving me alone with Mr. Smith. I told him I wanted to finish one last problem, and he soon left the room.

For reasons I'll never know, I decided to try to clean up the puddle, and two trips to the bathroom for paper towels got most of it up. I still had to walk three-quarters of a mile home and get into my house without being seen. It was almost dark as I left the school building, and though I would be able to make the journey without anyone spotting my completely soaked trousers, it also made the walk home extremely cold and most uncomfortable. My mother was up in her bedroom, making it easy to slip in and climb to the third floor unnoticed. A shower and dry clothes remedied the immediate problem, but my thoughts quickly went to how I could avoid school the next day. Could I conjure up a believable ailment before morning?

Despite a sleepless night, I somehow got the courage to head to school. I will forever be thankful to the classmate who could have had great fun at my expense. He never uttered a word to me, and the incident passed. I was spared public humiliation. I sensed that he somehow knew this was a subject better laid to rest. He was somewhat of a friend and must have sensed my anguish. However, the humiliation I felt persisted, and I never told anyone, family included, of the incident. Years later, when I became a teacher, my bathroom policy was put forth explicitly on day one: if one has to go, don't bother to raise a hand—just run. Do not pass Go; do not collect $200. Often, I would have a principal concerned that students were abusing bathroom privileges. They would say, "only one student at a time and with a signed pass." That day years earlier, when the dam started to break, waiting for a signed pass would not have worked. I incurred the wrath of an administrator on a couple of occasions, but that was small potatoes. No student of mine was going to suffer the humiliation I did.

In hindsight, I must have asked myself a hundred times why I didn't just run out of the room. It's hard to believe that the fear of getting in trouble would trump the embarrassment I would then endure. Teachers, to keep discipline, will impose a classroom climate to keep even the most challenging student in line, forgetting that this is overkill for some of the students in the class. A difficult or academically aggressive student will get the teacher's attention, but a shy child often gets lost or even hurt in the bustle of activity.

Middle school is a challenging time for any student, part of the reason I chose that age to teach. One never hears anyone saying they would like to return to the wonderful, carefree days of middle school. I was fragile at that point in my life and needed something to pad my ego. That did not happen; a part of me died that terrible afternoon.

THE TOY CHEST

I remember it well, a varnished wooden chest with something paint-ed on the lid, Donald Duck if my memory serves me correctly ... and it often doesn't. It had been mine as a child and was a wonder-ful place to store stuffed animals, baseball cards, and random toys. It served its purpose when I was sent to my room to clean up. I would be told I had an hour to clean up the mess in my room, and it would be inspected before I could go out to play ball. Like many children, once I got to my room, I would soon be distracted by some gadget, book, or game, and the hour would quickly pass. I would hear my father's foot-steps as he started up for the inspection. He still had a vestige of his military years and loved the inspector general role. With the sound of the first footstep, panic would set in, but fortunately, I was on the third floor. There would be time. Opening the lid to the toy chest, I would send toys and animals hurtling toward the chest. Kicking un-der the bed, anything that did not fit in the chest, I would be sitting on the chest as my father entered the room. He would compliment me on the clean-up job, never looking into the large chest. He must have known.

Time passed, the stuffed animals moved on, the baseball cards were thrown away, and a bookshelf became a more appropriate piece of furniture. The chest moved on to my brother Bill, four years young-er. He, like I, found that no one ever went in the toy chest. If things weren't strewn over the floor, our parents could live with a cluttered chest. And there was no way to organize a chest anyway. More years passed, and Bill reached the age of twelve, although he still had a collection of childhood treasures. Then came that fateful day when my mother, for no explicable reason, decided to open the toy chest. Big Mistake!! No one was home that day to hear what must have been an epic scream. Did a mother's scream happen if no one was around to hear it? Knowing my mother and what she was looking at, the scream was undoubtedly heard in a neighboring state.

My brother Bill specialized in tormenting me. Like all middle siblings, he had to find a way to get attention, which he did with surprising ease. I was the oldest of four, and Bill was number three. Gussie, the sister between us, could get everyone's attention without even trying, and the youngest, Kim, was only with us for four years, and she won the Whirling Dervish Award hands down. My mother never knew what hit her, and there was never a dull day in the Radcliffe household. Birth afforded me the oldest brother status, and that role comes with both positives and negatives.

Bill and I were far enough apart in age to not compete, and I'm sure he looked up to his older brother in many ways. But, like any younger brother, he was an imp. He constantly searched for ways to get under my skin, and when he discovered something that worked, he applied it relentlessly with always the same outcome. I would finally break and react: close the door on him, push him away. After he reported my reaction, I would always get the same speech, "George, you're four years older, and you ought to know better."

To which I would reply, "But, he …."

My father's reply was predictable. "George, he's younger and doesn't know any better." Over the years, I impatiently waited for the time when Bill would "know better." He could throw a water balloon into my room, and I should have known better than to open the door. If he ran off with schoolwork I was working on, I shouldn't have had the papers out. It's not fair that a younger brother can hit an older brother, but the family won't allow for any retaliation. Why don't older brothers ever get a period when they are allowed not to know any better? I can't wait for senility to set in because I'll finally be able to tell everyone, "I don't know any better."

Anyway, I digress. I would have loved to see her reaction when she opened the toy chest. I can only imagine, but the fact that she was still in her bedroom sobbing several hours later tells us the initial shock must have been substantial. I was the first to go into her bedroom. There was no "How was school today?" to which I could thoughtfully respond, "Fine." There was only sobbing. Had someone died? I could see that the house was still intact, so someone's death seemed the logical cause. Since she wanted to be left alone, I closed the door and went to my room to do homework. When Gussie and Bill came home, I steered them away from my mother's room. The sobbing continued.

When my father arrived home that night, he went up into their bedroom as part of his usual "I'm home" routine. What seemed like an eternity passed. We were well past dinner time, and she had made no move toward the kitchen. None of us dared utter a comment; we all were thinking the worst. Finally, my father exited the room and called Bill. That seemed strange and did not fit at all with my death hypothesis. The conversation in the room became more agitated, and Gussie and I pretended not to listen. Every once in a while, the volume would increase to where the conversation was decipherable. Bill was clearly in deep doo-doo.

Twice we heard the words "toy chest" emanating from the room. Gussie and I looked at each other and quickly sprinted up the stairs to Bill's room. We usually respected the privacy of each other's rooms, but these circumstances warranted circumventing that rule. Gussie got to the chest first and lifted the lid. Her eyes grew wide with surprise. As I got to the chest, all suddenly became clear. No toys and baseball cards were in the chest … and no stuffed animals. Instead, the chest was filled to the brim with magazines, not just any magazines, but all *Playboys*. Gussie was giggling by this point and quickly flipping through one of the magazines. I had seen *Playboys* before, but I wasn't prepared to have my younger sister holding open a nude centerfold for me to see. I suggested we quickly leave the room; things were tense enough in that house.

No one spoke a word over dinner that night. Bill never once looked up from his plate, I tried my best to look uninformed, and Gussie unsuccessfully attempted to suppress an occasional giggle. My father tried artfully to talk about other subjects, but no one bit. Finally, Gussie could hold back no longer, "Bill, where did you get all those *Playboys*?" That's what was so wonderful about my sister; she was always blunt and to the point. I chose my words carefully to maintain my reputation as the responsible eldest sibling. Gussie was direct. I remember her once walking up to a rotund visitor and asking her why she was so fat. Gussie wore honesty like a badge of honor.

My mother seethed with anger at hearing the question, and Bill started to squirm in his seat. To the eldest son, this was great—some real family drama. After a bit of hesitation and without looking up, Bill said, "Grandfather gave them to me." That did it! No one expected that name to flow from his mouth. You see, our beloved grandfather was about ninety years old, and he was the last person in the world that anyone expected to have a *Playboy*. Was my brother really that stupid? Older brothers usually consider younger brothers a lower life form, but Bill had hit rock bottom. My mother started crying again and spoke about how lying to cover up a crime was often worse than the crime itself. If only Richard Nixon had listened to her. Much to my shock and surprise, Bill stuck to his story: his ninety-year-old dignified grandfather, known for being a voracious reader of classic and historical literature and who could not drive, was supplying him with *Playboys*. As bizarre and ridiculous as this story was, he didn't budge. After the meal, we retreated to our respective rooms, and my parents fled to their bedroom. Possessing the magazines was bad enough, but Bill tried to cover up his crime with a lie. Bill surprisingly seemed unconcerned. I was trying to figure out how to get one of the magazines out of the toy chest.

I remember thinking that evening that if I had been caught with the magazines, they would already be autopsying me at this point. As the oldest, I was seldom cut any slack. I was the trailblazer, preparing the way for my siblings. By the time they reached my age, they would be able to get away with far more than I did with much smaller consequences. My mother was wonderful and caring, but I sometimes felt (as many children do) that she was stuck back in the Middle Ages. At age fifteen, I had been reprimanded for seeing The Pink Panther with a friend. The movie was rated PG, and someone kisses someone in the film—scathing! And my brother, three years younger than me, had a truckload of magazines filled with naked women ... and he was still alive.

The next day Mom and Dad worked out a plan. Dad was not making much of this, but he was catering to my mother's extreme emotional reaction. Mom was going to take Bill to see a priest. I didn't know they still did exorcisms! I was to accompany her and Bill on the adventure. Bill was irritated that he had to give up a day but still seemed remarkably calm. I couldn't wait to see how this would play out. No one spoke on the short ride to the Cathedral of Mary Our Queen. We entered the rectory and waited while the secretary went to get the priest; Mom was tense, to say the least.

We were ushered into a room where we were asked to have a seat. The priest led Mom into another room and closed the door. I looked over at Bill, who once again seemed calm. A window in the door separated us from the meeting, and we could hear every word spoken. Mom, sobbing periodically, recounted the whole tale. She expected a monstrous reaction to this dastardly deed, but the priest just listened calmly.

"Father, these magazines were full of pictures of ... well, naked women,"

"Yes, Augusta, I know."

"But in the center of the magazine is this large picture that is ...." She tried to show with her hands how large the photo was.

Father quickly corrected her, saying, "No, Augusta, the centerfold is only this big."

Mom, sobbing again, said, "But father, he's only twelve."

"Augusta, he's as normal as can be. It's just natural boyish curiosity. He will turn out simply fine. I thought when you called that Bill was in serious trouble."

"But he's so young."

"Gus, he's a normal twelve-year-old and, from what I could see, a wonderful child."

Bill was grinning from ear to ear at this point; salvation came from a place he never expected. I sat there in disbelief. I had envisioned the incredible punishment my brother would receive, and the chances for that were dwindling fast. The meeting ended shortly, and Father came out to give my brother a pat on the back. And I got in trouble for going to *The Pink Panther*? Nothing much was said after that meeting. I always wondered what became of those magazines but never broached the subject. I was amazed and impressed that Bill had not buckled under pressure. He had stuck to his story right to the end. But getting them from my grandfather? I needed to counsel my brother to be less creative with his stories. However, at least he didn't blame it on me.

Later that year, I was down helping my grandfather with a cleaning project. His house was a veritable museum with every room filled floor to ceiling with everything imaginable. Exploring the house was an adventure; one never knew what would turn up next. He sent me upstairs with a load of old Christmas magazines he had collected over the years, and I was to put them in a particular closet. Musty was the odor of choice throughout the house, but this closet took it to another level. These magazines were from the nineteenth century, and I was fascinated by the old advertisements. As I found the proper place for them in the closet, I set them down and turned to leave. There, sitting in another corner, were several *Playboys*.

ORNITHOLOGY AND ENTOMOLOGY
FOR UNINFORMED MALES

A pivotal moment in the relationship between a father and son comes when the father feels that the time has arrived to lay out the facts of life; this usually occurs years after the son has figured out all the particulars of sex, or at least thinks he has. It can become an unproductive and often embarrassing moment for both of them. As a father, I won no awards in this department, leaking bits of information along the way and assuming my sons were correctly filling in all the pieces.

Sex is an awkward subject between the two generations, to begin with, and I pray that the increased openness today is at least partially rectifying the situation. When I grew up, a child could reach well into the teens before putting all the pieces together. Couples on TV shows slept in separate beds (as did my parents in those days), kisses could only last a few seconds, and any references to the acts that led to procreation were censored.

Later on, I wondered how I had been created since every child in my generation knew that their parents couldn't have ever engaged in sexual intercourse. Immaculate conception seemed the only avenue to birth for those in the Baby Boomer generation. So how, after all of this, could a parent engage in the subject with a child? For obvious biological reasons, girls got much better parent support, but boys were left to the wolves ... cleverly disguised as their friends. Peers, claiming to be informed, and some pathetic "dirty jokes" left me more confused than ever. I didn't live in the country and had never seen any animal give birth. How was I to know?

However, I was a reasonably bright and curious kid. Since I had a sister somewhat the same age, it did occur to me that she had come down the pipe incomplete, clearly missing one prominent organ. My mother had these protrusions on her chest, which my father did not, but no one ever told me their function. Since I had never seen a mother nursing a child, I figured they had been added to help distinguish women from men or boost the bra industry. No one was sharing any information, and I sure was not going to ask. As I reached a slightly higher level of mental processing, I decided it was time to try to figure it out myself.

Until that point, the answer was obvious; babies came from hospitals. At age eight, my mother went to the hospital empty-handed and came home with a child. Somehow, I missed the whole weight gain thing. However, in a moment of sheer genius, I started wondering where the hospital was getting all these babies. Disney cartoons showed storks flying babies in, but I knew storks were not indigenous to our area. Surely, a friend or I would have seen an incoming stork and child at some point. The phrase "the birds and the bees" clearly leaves questions unanswered for mammals. And no one ever bothered to tell me what birds and bees did; was flying somehow a part of the process? That would undoubtedly make sex exciting, but I knew my parents couldn't get off the ground. I had tried strapping boards to my arms with no success, and my first parachuting attempt off our porch with a sheet had left me with a sprained ankle.

So, it was time for me to figure this out for myself. In those days, no one in their right mind would have let eight-year-olds access any written information, and my parents had done an admirable job of dropping no clues. I was reading the Hardy Boys mysteries at that point, and this would be a job for an able detective. Then a friend of my parents let slip the first big clue, asking my mother after my sister's arrival if she was glad to have her body back to herself. That comment sent me off to ponder the possibilities. After a couple of sleepless nights, I finally decided that my sister had been inside of my mother. As shocking and improbable as that was, it became the best-case hypothesis. Of course, there were two significant obstacles to accepting this theory. How had my sister gotten in there, and even more incomprehensible, how had she gotten out?

It was time to hit the World Book Encyclopedia. Being the genius that I was, I went to the human anatomy section, not anything having to do with reproduction. I was going to figure out how my sister had gotten out. After careful study, I found three possibilities: the mouth, vagina, and anus. I could quickly rule out the mouth as it didn't seem a mother "threw up" to get her child out. Also, after gagging on the monstrous lumps in my mother's oatmeal all these years, I knew no mother in her right mind would get the child out this way. That left the two posterior openings, and both seemed equally unlikely. No kid could get out of those little openings. After weeks of stewing on this question, it was time to go to a higher authority, my friend Jack. He claimed to be the font of all knowledge and would provide the answer.

Jack quickly confirmed that the child did come from inside the mother. I had gotten that part right! She took a baby pill, and after the baby grew, she sat on the "john" one night with the baby suddenly popping out. Ah, so it was coming out the rectum; although having been constipated on one occasion, that seemed a painful way to give birth. His answer left a few questions, however. Couldn't the mother accidentally flush the child down the toilet? And why go to the hospital since every home has a bathroom? And how did they get it out of the bottom of the outhouse before there were toilets? Jack wasn't ready to have his infinite wisdom tested by a couple of questions, but he offered further information. Mothers needed to give birth in the hospital because the doctor needed to "clean up" the baby. That made perfect sense since any baby being ejected from the rectum would need a thorough cleaning.

With everything finally answered, I went home delighted... that was until the following day. With breakfast every morning, my mother gave me vitamins in liquid form, but this particular morning, she handed me a pill for the first time. I had never heard of a man going to the hospital to have a baby, but they had an anus, too. And now Mom was handing me a strange pill! I wanted to believe it was a vitamin pill, but I had never seen my father take one. Was I now going to have to check out the contents of the toilet bowl every time I defecated? I liked to worry, but this was more than my young brain could process. Thankfully, my father was also taking a vitamin pill for the first time that morning, and I knew he was NOT going to have a child. Relieved, I popped the tablet down, but I knew I would have to be careful whenever someone wanted to give me a pill.

Thankfully, I soon made friends with a boy named Frank, who lived in the country. He had seen several farm animals born, and they didn't come out of the rectum. By process of elimination, they had to have come out of the vagina, and to the best of my knowledge, I didn't have one. I would never have to give birth. What a relief! But what would happen if a baby somehow got in there; there would be no way to get it out. Frank had that all figured out as his family had once owned an animal where they had to surgically remove the young when the mother could not give birth. The pieces were all starting to come together finally. I often wondered whether my parents would have answered any questions if I had asked, but I wasn't going to embarrass myself by trying.

It had still never occurred to this brilliant young scientist that the male had anything to do with it, and, for a while, I thought I had it all figured out. One thing dogged me, however. Why did males have a penis while females did not? Frank told me one day that the male has to get the entire process started with his penis. This was crazy since, as a ten-year-old, I knew that only urine came out of the penis. More confused than ever, I pressed him for details. "You mean the man urinates into the woman?" Gross! That was apparently how it all happened, but women urinated, too. The more I learned, the more confused I became. No information came from my parents, and schools were not touching on the subject. What would have happened if Adam had not urinated into Eve, and why would she have ever allowed him anyway? This just made no sense. God was supposed to be this bright guy, but he created the dumbest way imaginable to produce a baby. There had to be more to the story, or maybe my friends weren't as brilliant as they thought.

Somehow, I pieced the process together between ten and fourteen, although it still seemed remarkably flawed and incomplete. Soon after came the big talk, the one I never thought would happen. My father and I were raking leaves that fall day.

"George, I've been meaning to talk with you."

"What about, Dad?"

After an exceptionally long pause, he finally asked, "Have you noticed that men and women are different?"

"Yes." Did he think I was stupid or something? Where was this conversation headed?

"Have you ever wondered why they are different?"

"Yes."

Another long pause. He clearly needed help with the conversation, but my one-word responses left him floundering. We continued raking with neither saying anything. I was wondering what was coming next, and I'm sure his carefully planned comments had unraveled entirely at this point. I was surprised at how nervous he seemed; after all, wasn't I supposed to be the nervous one? And he was a lawyer— they don't get worried.

Finally, "Do you know where babies come from?"

"Yes." I couldn't let on that I was still a little confused, but I was a grown-up fourteen-year-old.

"And you know that males have a penis." In my fourteen years of life, I had noticed that I had that organ.

"And females don't have one."

"Yes." He was now searching for the next question, and after a long pause, "Do you have any questions?"

"No." This was now a strategic chess match, and I unintentionally blocked his every move. This was his job as a parent, and I certainly wasn't going to volunteer any information since I might be wrong.

"Well ... you know that men and women are different. Your mother and I are different." My father was a bright man, but he was flunking his Mensa exam this day.

"I know."

"Well ... um ... have you ... um ... ever wondered ...?"

My mother's voice rang out from the house, "George, you're wanted on the phone." Both my father and I were named George, but we always knew which one she was calling for by the tone of my mother's voice. He walked inside, and I went back to raking leaves. A good ten minutes passed before he returned. I awaited the next question in this painful conversation.

After some vigorous raking and a long pause, he finally asked. "Do you think the Colts can take care of the Packers tomorrow?" Happily, for both of us, we were back to normal.

Years later, as a father, I vowed to do a better job. I didn't. I made small feeble attempts with my three boys to ensure they got the basics right. I had decided that my kids would at least get the terminology right. They were not going to "wee-wee" with their "pee-pee" or worry about which excretory function was a #1 or a #2. I remember sharing with one that "defecation" was a more appropriate term for "pooping," only to have his pre-school teacher get upset when he asked to "defecate". That same year, he came home asking what a "pussy" was.

Correctly assuming this wasn't a question about cats, I sat down with all three and explained that the correct term was "vagina." Knowing that most of their friends would not use the proper term, I wrote the word out for them. I then figured that if they could spell the word, it would stick for all time. So, we practiced the spelling, and they made the spelling into a simple song for some unknown reason. They would have this term mastered—no more misconceptions or innocently inappropriate language.

Later that afternoon, the five of us went grocery shopping before going out for a simple dinner. Even though the boys were young, we always let them assist, sending them looking for one item after another. They would charge off to the next aisle to retrieve a box of spaghetti or a can of beans. We knew they were well capable of getting into minor trouble, but we wanted to teach them how to help and be responsible. I could hear them giggling in the next aisle, and that's when it started. I suddenly heard them singing loudly, "V-A-G-I-N-A, vagina, vagina, V-A-G-I-N-A, vagina, vagina." Leaving my cart, I quickly raced down my aisle and around the corner. Getting to the next aisle, I noticed that they had paraded to the end of that aisle and were rounding the corner. Across the store, I could hear the song continuing, "V-A-G-I-N-A, vagina, vagina, V-A-G-I-N-A, vagina, vagina." As I sprinted down the aisle, hoping this was all going unnoticed, I passed an older woman who looked terrified as she gazed at the threesome. I slowed down as I passed her, lest she think I was somehow connected to these anatomical troubadours. Finally catching up to them, I managed to get them to lower their voices. Trying to get them to change the subject without further dignifying the song, I added, "How about those Orioles?"

I THOUGHT GOD WAS
AN OLD WHITE GUY

At the age of six, I sat for the first time in the dining room of Spocott, the ancestral family farmhouse, feeling as if I had been transported back in time. My grandfather had filled me with stories of this 360-year-old home and our family: making peace with the Native Americans around the historic Council Oak near the house, building schooners that traveled the globe, the unique, self-sufficient community which inhabited the property for a century. The house even smelled old, and my mother, quite the city girl, found it hard to smile as she encountered and battled mice, black snakes, and an army of flies. The original ceiling beams defined the room, and the massive fireplace told its own story of many a winter meal. The room was adorned with relics of the past: pewter plates and candlesticks, an old clock on the mantle, a bride's ball used to carry fire to "jump-start" a new dwelling fireplace, molds for making bayberry candles years ago, and artifacts related to the shipbuilding which had ceased almost 100 years prior. What was unusual was that with all the history embedded in this home, only one picture adorned the walls of this room, that of a young Black woman. To a young child who had been raised in an all-white world, the picture was puzzling. Why would someone hang a picture of their "maid" in this historic house? Who was she, and why had she been granted this significant status? As I was to find out, this picture was of no ordinary woman. Adaline Morris Wheatley, or

"Aunt Adaline," as all had called her, kept watch over this room for over sixty years as a cook, nurse, honorary family member, and one who helped raise my grandfather. My prejudice was showing, and I had much to learn.

While I was raised by parents who certainly respected all races and religions, I still grew up in a white world. In my Christian education, God, Jesus, Mary, and all the saints were portrayed as white, but so were virtually all of the heroes and celebrities I encountered. Superman and Batman were white, as were every U.S. president, all the Disney princesses, Santa Claus, and virtually every movie star. My Oz was a 100% white community: our neighborhood was white even though there was no "whites only" sign at the beginning of the road, I went to a school with no minorities, and I attended a church with only white parishioners. I had no frame of reference to accurately judge the world in which I lived.

Our family watched the evening news regularly once we acquired a television set, and race issues were starting to make headlines. I was born in 1949 and was too young to be aware of the 1954 Brown vs. Board of Education ruling or the Montgomery Bus Boycott and Rosa Parks the following year. However, in 1957 when President Eisenhower sent troops into Little Rock, Arkansas, to enforce integration, I took notice. However, living in a completely white world made this news seem distant, as if occurring on the other side of the globe. I saw my parents express disgust when Governor Faubus blocked Black students from entering their school. Still, I had no frame of reference to understand and empathize with what was happening since the only Black I encountered personally was Beatrice, the marvelous nurse and house cleaner my parents had hired. She was young, intelligent, and a valuable part of our family. She could cook, clean when needed, and care for my sisters, Kim and Gussie, both of whom had significant medical problems. Beatrice was the first Black I knew well; our family couldn't have survived without her. However,

I sometimes felt awkward around her because I had no experience with her world. It was impossible for a young child growing up in that white world to understand the racism that had caused there to be two worlds, one for whites and one for everyone else. I had no context to understand poverty, prejudice, and lack of opportunity. However, the white world, the only world I knew, began to thankfully crumble, but it would take time.

I remember walking in on Beatrice and Gussie watching a soap opera one afternoon around Christmas. One of the characters was playing Santa Claus, and Gussie, never shy or at a loss for words, asked Beatrice if Santa Claus came to her house. I had always assumed that Santa was color blind and visited all, but Beatrice's response surprised me. "Sure, he comes to our house, but our Santa is colored." Blacks in the 1950s were referred to as colored, a term which thankfully was soon put to rest. The term always bothered me as a child since my crayon box also had a flesh-colored crayon; weren't we all colored? She then preceded to say that her God was also colored. I remember thinking a lot that night about how wrong it was that God, Christ, Santa, and Superman were always portrayed as white. While that didn't seem to bother Beatrice, it seemed wrong to me. As silly as that short conversation was, it forced me to ask many questions and, for the first time, seriously question the world that had been presented to me.

There were two kinds of jokes prevalent during that period. They were similar in that each belittled a group of people. They began:

"There was a Protestant, Catholic, and Jew ...."

"There was a white man, a colored man, and a Jew ...."

My parents had some friends who often shared one of these jokes. They were demeaning to Blacks, Jews, and Catholics to a lesser extent. I was Catholic but never took offense, and since my parents had a few Jewish friends, I could never understand why they were the butt of the jokes. The ones insulting Blacks were the most offensive; this was my first introduction to racism. While I had limited experience interacting with Blacks, I knew the jokes were inappropriate, and my parents were the reason for that. My father did not tell jokes; he told wonderful humorous stories that stemmed from his past and those of people he knew. He never once told a story that belittled anyone unless he was poking fun at himself, which he often did.

I found most jokes humorless compared to my father's stories, where the humor came from the silly everyday things that happen to us. Getting to know my grandfather showed where my father had gotten his sense of humor. Both, as did my mother, had a profound respect for the humanity of all, and, whether they meant to or not, they gave me a framework for respecting all and never making anyone, except themselves, the subject of a joke. Even though I was growing up in a predominantly white world, they were teaching me how to deal with a more diverse world when times would change enough to allow it. When the Polish or Polack jokes surfaced years later, I instantly rejected them as offensive and ridiculous. Once again, they showed no imagination; anyone can tell a cruel joke or hurl an insult for comic effect, but telling a story that finds humor in the everyday moments in life or pokes fun at oneself requires much greater skill and imagination.

I did tell offensive jokes, only offensive if you were an elephant. I'm probably the only person who found these funny, and they bothered no one—although many never could see their humor. To me, they were anti-jokes, in many ways poking fun at the offensive and stupid jokes that so many told.

"Why did the elephant wear green tennis shoes?

"*To hide in the grass.*"

"Why did the elephant wear pink tennis shoes?"

"*The green ones were in the wash.*"

"How can you tell if an elephant has been in your refrigerator?"

"*By the footprints in the Jell-O.*"

I'll spare you the rest.

Failing to find the jokes of many funny also contributed to my feeling of not fitting in. In high school, I would uncomfortably listen in on a typical teenage "dirty" joke and, in some cases, even not understand it. Having two sisters I cared deeply for, I found those jokes demeaning to them and other girls. I had one relative who would tell racially inappropriate jokes, and these bothered me, although I never spoke up. My father had an effective way of dealing with this— quickly change the subject. He also often talked about his experiences in World War II as an aircraft maintenance officer. In encountering racism here, he found that laws and regulations were often more of a problem than the soldiers themselves. He spoke fondly of the Black officers and enlistees he worked with, some of whom were even better educated than the whites, but regulations often restricted the positions they could hold. On one bus trip, he and other whites were prohibited from sitting with a Black friend, who was relegated to the back of the bus. These experiences left an impression on him, and his stories were one of my first introductions to the racism still existing in the world. I heard about it in the news, but his stories were real to me. However, my world was white, and the limited integration of our school while I was in high school still left no significant contact with Blacks and other ethnic groups.

That would change dramatically during my junior year because of one remarkable individual. We had a religion class in the school, and the Catholics were taught separately by a seminarian training to be a priest. Jay had a unique viewpoint as he grew up in a rough area and briefly served time in prison. Although white, he was a dramatic change from the usual white society I encountered daily. On one occasion, in a discussion, he lost patience with several in the class who, although not racist, were spouting a degree of arrogance. Jay countered their arguments for a while and then said there was something he wanted to show us if any were willing to join him for a church service on Sunday. My life certainly lacked excitement, and I volunteered to join him.

That Sunday, several met him at the school, and he loaded us into his van, driving us downtown into an area of the inner city we were unfamiliar with. We parked and walked a couple of blocks to a small church. I was stunned when we entered the church; there was not a white face anywhere. Jay had been there before as several parishioners acknowledged his entrance. I felt like all eyes were on me, which I found quite uncomfortable.

We found a place to sit, still noticing many glancing in our direction. Other than the sea of Black faces, this seemed like an ordinary church, and, of course, the service began in the same way, but that's where any similarity ended. Usually, a church service for me was monotonous at best, with the sermon the only variation, and this was usually just an elaboration or interpretation of the gospel. Thus, for me, a service was just an hour for daydreaming and people-watching. This day, however, I was in for a shock. The parishioners actually sang! This small group made ten times the noise of those in the monstrous cathedral I usually attended, where only a handful of people sang with the others just mouthing the words. I remember looking around the church and noticing that these people wanted to be there and took the hymns and service seriously. The sermon was not the usual monotonous college lecture but an impassioned plea for people to change their lives; no one was sleeping through it or looking at their watch.

I soon forgot about my discomfort and just took in all that was happening in the church. It was the quickest church service I had ever experienced, and what happened afterward was even more noteworthy. Several parishioners came up to talk to Jay and engaged us in conversation. I went from feeling awkward to enjoying the situation. So often, after a service, all would take off in separate directions, but these people were one big family, staying to chat, laugh, hug, and celebrate.

Several profound things happened that morning. I got to feel the extreme discomfort of being a minority, if even for just a brief moment, and I felt the warmth of a church community I had never experienced before. For a brief moment, I was ashamed to be white. While I knew my Oz was not the real world, I was still extremely comfortable living in it. One brief experience hardly qualifies as a life-changing moment, but it reinforced my parents' picture of a world free of prejudice. What I still could not see or understand was how many minorities had justification for feeling anger and resentment for years of limited opportunity in a country that was supposedly a home for all. I saw no anger that day.

I thought back to the conversation Gussie and I had with Beatrice years earlier. She also bore no resentment. While I lived in a white world, she saw the world through her glasses. It would still be a few years before I saw a Black Santa Claus and many years before there would be a Black superhero, but I was well on my way to discarding the old, bearded, white guy image of a creator. People should be able to create whatever image of a deity fits them. Being a Catholic, I didn't see the acceptance of other viewpoints and beliefs that was needed. I loved my mother dearly, but hearing from her that only Catholics went to heaven didn't sit well with me since we had an Episcopalian father. I realized that my Oz was an artificial world and that the real world was far more diverse, wondrous, and exciting. I wonder how much more I could have learned if I had grown up in a more diverse environment.

FIFTY MILES OF TOILET PAPER

My mother was a child of the Great Depression. While we have had recessions and economic downturns since then, nothing compared to the depression this country endured in the years following the stock market crash of 1929. Banks collapsed, many lost all their savings and jobs, "bankruptcy" became the most used word in daily papers, and suicides skyrocketed. My mother, the oldest of four children, was five. Her father had been living on his father's investments, and the family wealth quickly evaporated. With no reliable source of income, her family endured challenging times, and during the next five to ten years, she and her family lived a meager existence. They kept their house, could afford essential clothing, and had food on the table for every meal. In other words, they were "well off" compared to many. They did not suffer, but she experienced a lifestyle grounded in conservation, reuse, and careful fiscal planning. "Waste" was not in her family's vocabulary, and sacrifice was the norm. There were no fancy clothes, expensive toys, or vacations. In a family built on love, these were easy sacrifices to make.

She often spoke of a special occasion, which occurred once or twice yearly; the family would throw caution to the wind and splurge. They would pile in a car, drive less than one mile to the store, and purchase a pint of ice cream. The six would then share the treat. Today most individuals can easily stomach a pint of ice cream in one sitting without help. Sharing that pint might explain my mother's obsession with this frozen dairy product in later years. These years of depression were followed by World War II, where conservation, sacrifice, and rationing were the backbone of every American's existence. I wonder how many would happily tolerate this today when so many of us have been spoiled. My mother not only never forgot these lessons but wore them as a badge of honor her entire life—and evolved this behavior into an art form rarely matched.

Going out to dinner in my later years with my mother was an adventure. She always carried a large purse, and history may record this as the origin of the doggie bag. She would always ask for more dinner rolls even when everyone was too full to eat at this point, and into the purse, they would go along with every scrap of excess food, extra butter, creamers, sugar packs, and matches. She may have single-handedly increased the cost of restaurant meals over the years. In her later years at a retirement home, the dessert would come with the meal. She would persuade the waiter to give her a second scoop of ice cream in a take-out cup, and soon they would automatically bring her several scoops. In her last couple of years there, she and my father managed to pay for only dinners each day but left with enough food for breakfasts and most lunches.

However, I saw this art form's true development in my childhood. Mom learned that buying in bulk was cheaper. Now, as my wife will tell you, I engage in this activity to an extent. I am a cheapskate, but Mom took it to heights never envisioned by any on the planet. Our kitchen was always well-stocked, and we soon purchased an extra freezer to store frozen items on sale. But I knew we had turned the corner when I came home from school one day, going to the pantry for a snack. The door only opened part way, and I soon found out the cause of the obstruction. Mom had discovered a brand of diet soda on sale and learned she could save a penny a can by buying in quantity. Quantity to Mom did not mean a case of soda but twenty cases. She had ordered so much (all that the store carried) that they delivered it to our home. In the early days of diet soda, cans were "more primitive" than today. The steel cans gave the soda a metallic taste, and one needed a can opener to open the can in two places (the second hole to release the vacuum).

We soon found that this diet soda had issues; oh, did it ever! Or should I say it caused issues? I'm unsure what chemistry was at play here, but these sodas meant "party time" for her intestinal bacteria. My friends always knew when my mother was home from the sonic blasts from elsewhere in the house. The carbonation process must have been different then because one would be belching prolifically for the first five minutes of consumption. I was scolded for daring to put an elbow on the table by my mother, whose words were punctuated by repeated belching. I never quite understood why a random elbow was more offensive than the gastric blasts that became too common. Within fifteen minutes, the intestinal blasting would begin, leading to my misconception that flatulation resulted from carbonated beverages shooting through one's alimentary canal.

The drinks were tasteless as artificial sweeteners were in their infancy, and we soon found that they quickly lost their carbonation in the can. Before Mom had consumed half of the cases, they had all gone flat. A Depression child does not waste anything, anytime; "Thou shalt not waste" is the commandment that comes before "Thou shalt not steal." Additionally, disposing of any product would destroy her "look at how much I saved" argument; at a penny a can, we did save $4.80, although we spent more than that on house air fresheners throughout the consumption. She eventually decided that she needed help consuming the remaining cases. Our supply of real Coca-Cola now dried up, and we were told we needed to help finish the supply of diet soda first. There were two flavors of this generic chemical concoction—cola and orange-flavored. They tasted the same, and were it not for the color of the can, one would never know which one they were consuming. Completely flat, it also bore no resemblance to the soda I loved; it was a cross between cleaning fluid and my childhood chemistry experiments. Somehow, our family finished it all, just in time for sale number two.

This was a sale on tomato juice. I have no idea what she saved on this deal, but coming home from school that day, I saw twenty-four quarts of tomato juice on the counter. Now I loved tomato juice, but eight to nine quarts into the bonanza, it started losing its appeal, not to mention the intestinal effects of consuming large glasses of the stuff. About the time we were halfway through this reservoir of juice, it started to go bad. Now my mother was stuck in a tricky situation. Should she admit defeat, suck in her loss, and deep-six the remainder, or should she fill her family with souring juice? In the beginning, she was clearly in denial. The rest of us kept commenting on the bitter taste, but she told us that it tasted simply fine. The night my sister vomited a glass of juice all over the family's recently cleaned beige carpet gave Mom the real slap she needed. With tears in her eyes, she poured seven quarts of tomato juice down the drain. I assumed that Mom had learned her lesson about sales, but the tomato juice debacle inspired her for her magnum opus.

I remember that fateful day well. I walked into the house with a friend, and we started to head up to my room to listen to records. Giving my well-rehearsed "school was fine" line to Mom, I was ready to exit stage right when she casually mentioned that there was something in my room she wanted to store in there. I mumbled my usual teenage "OK" and headed up the stairs. When I opened the door to my bedroom, I saw two boxes, each large enough to hold a washing machine. I initially got excited; possibly this was some great new "toy" for the family: pool or ping pong table, entertainment system, or a new bicycle. My friend and I tore into the boxes, and he saw "it" first. Falling on the floor in laughter, he soon dissolved into hysterical cackling. I soon saw what precipitated his reaction and stared at "it" in total disbelief. I was NOT laughing. This had to be a joke, but my

mother did not have that sense of humor. The boxes were full of ...,
and I mean packed full of ... toilet paper ... 500 rolls to be exact. My
friend knew my family was a bit out of the ordinary, but how does
one explain 500 rolls of toilet paper? It came in assorted colors, and
there was likely enough dye in those boxes to set the Chesapeake Bay
restoration back ten years.

The word quickly spread among my limited social set. "You must
see what's in George's room; you won't believe it!" There was nowhere
else in the house to store the rolls. It might mildew in the basement,
but my room became the sacred depository since I had two closets. I
filled one closet floor to ceiling with the rolls, but that took only one
of the boxes. I had to empty the second closet of many of my clothes
to store the contents of the second box. Now, not only did anyone
in the house needing toilet paper enter my room without knocking
(one doesn't knock if one has to go), but my closets saw more gaping
visitors than if there had been a mummy in them. Fifteen-year-olds
have a difficult enough time without being known as the "guy whose
bedroom is full of toilet paper." I was never going to be a "big man
on campus," but 500 rolls of TP in one's room surely is an automatic
disqualification. However, my bedroom did become a popular tourist
attraction; I should have charged admission.

Several weeks before graduation, the last roll finally disappeared.
We should have brought in a brass band to help celebrate the mo-
mentous occasion, and I would have set off fireworks if they had been
allowed. I often wondered what people thought of "the bedroom
filled with toilet paper." Did our family have a toilet paper fetish?
Was there a genetic abnormality in our family affecting intestinal
function? Or was I just bizarre? My mother saved a penny a roll, but
I would gladly have paid the five dollars saved to avoid the humiliation of being the "toilet paper guy." Why hadn't the sale been on a
case of potato chips or cookies? Now I appreciated toilet paper, especially after hearing my grandfather's stories about the barrel of corn

cobs outside his family's outhouse. But 500 rolls? That's almost fifty miles—I had been disturbed enough to do the math. Our poor septic system! My poor room!

Now I must confess that I do stockpile sale items up to a point. I pinch pennies and can't stand wasting food. And I will always bend over to pick up a penny. It's not about economics, although I hate to waste money. It must be genetic, but nothing in my DNA would ever send me out to buy a lifetime supply of toilet paper. Mom passed away eight years ago, and while I remember her fondly, I have to admit I thought a tombstone shaped like a roll of toilet paper would be fitting. Alas, I passed on those ideas because a regular stone was so much cheaper. I sit here now with a hole in one of my socks and a ripped pair of pants. I am not a child of the Great Depression, but I am my mother's son.

Now that my mother has passed, I wonder if storing all that toilet paper in my room was just her way of testing me to strengthen my character. In those years, I learned to take considerable ribbing and eventually could laugh at the situation. I want to think that was her motivation, but then with all that horrid diet soda, maybe we did need that much toilet paper.

I CAN DRIVE!

September 14, 1965, was a special day; turning sixteen meant I had arrived, or so I thought. I'd run for cover if I met the sixteen-year-old version of myself on the street today. But that day, I was king of the world even though just one day older than the fifteen-year-old, so lacking in self-confidence and wisdom. But at sixteen, I could get a license and drive—power, freedom! With a permit, I would no longer have to be chauffeured around by my mother, which would surely raise my standing in my minimal social world. I loved my mom, but this was the woman who still tried to comb my hair in public. How can one achieve respectability in today's world being driven around by a comb-wielding mother?

My father wisely decided to enroll me as a student driver with a local company. This was before the mandatory driver's ed course; drive around with an instructor until he felt you were ready to take the test. Mr. Stevens drove a tank rather than a car. This was a blessing, as I quickly learned to navigate tight corners on small side streets. The car also had great acceleration, and since we lived three blocks from the Jones Falls Expressway, Baltimore's version of the Indianapolis Speedway, this was a positive asset. It was a bit bizarre driving a car where the passenger also had a steering wheel; so much for trusting me, but Mr. Stevens was sitting back with hands nowhere near the wheel. We drove through neighborhood after neighborhood with an occasional terrifying foray onto the Expressway, but all was going well. It's hard to gain too much confidence when one is only in possession of a learner's permit.

To my father's credit, he had beautifully prepared me for driving. As he put it, driving was not turning the wheel and pushing pedals; it was avoiding all the idiots on the road. He would often put me in the front seat and have me anticipate problems: a child about to run out between two parked cars, a driver running a red light, or a person tailgating. I would look ahead, telling him what potential problems could occur. He also made me navigate with a map, anticipating turns and always knowing what direction we were driving and where our ultimate destination resided. Looking back, I realize what genius this was—to learn these skills before one was behind the wheel of a car. I wonder how well kids learn this today between GPS unit proliferation and the cell phones that get too much attention. To this day, those are some of the most valuable skills I have ever learned. It's hard to get lost if one always knows what direction they are headed, and I'm too proud (or should I say stubborn) to use a GPS unit. In over 50 years, I have never had an accident. Part of that is luck, but my father's teaching me to anticipate has played a significant role.

Part of my driver's training meant practicing driving with my parents. This was necessary but, at times, a mistake. While my father was calm and relaxed, with him even falling asleep once as he and I drove from Baltimore down to Cambridge, driving with Mom was an adventure. A true worrier, like any good mother, she could not have been tenser if she had been facing a firing squad. I remember one incident where we drove down a major thoroughfare in Baltimore, about to make a right-hand turn. I could see the turn far ahead with a car waiting at the stop sign. I put my blinker on well before the turn but had not even slowed down when Mom let out a blood-curdling scream that surely awoke every soul in every Baltimore cemetery. At the same time, she reached over, grabbed my arm, and dug her fingers down to my bone. I slammed on the brakes and somehow got the car to the side of the road. Puzzled and still looking around for the cause of the scream, I asked, "What is it, Mom?"

"There's a car at the stop sign!"

"I know; I saw it."

"But it might have pulled out in front of you."

"Mom ... I'm turning anyway."

"Oh."

From then on, she sat in the back seat if I had to drive with her. And my friends wouldn't see her sitting back there because chauffeuring one's mother around was not the way to get a ticket to Cooldom.

I passed the driving test with flying colors, but it took place on a flat surface. The test was no more a preparation for driving than jumping off a curb for skydiving. They need to add some rugged hills to the driving course to make it a real test. A person can think they know how to drive until they are sitting at a light at the top of a hill in a car with a manual transmission, knowing that by the time you get your foot off the brake and get the car in gear, the vehicle will have backed down the hill and into the Baltimore Harbor. I remember the cursed day vividly. I was sitting at a light in downtown Baltimore, sweating profusely since I was headed uphill on a steep slope. I had planned the move thoroughly; I had the car in gear and would quickly move my right foot from the brake to the accelerator while quickly lifting my left foot off the clutch to get moving before I rolled backward. It seemed so easy in my head, no problem! There was thankfully no car behind me because the traffic was backed up at the previous light. Maybe I could get a green light before the wave of traffic reached me, but, alas, this was an area of Baltimore where lights were synchronized. The wave rolled up behind me before the light turned. Suddenly it turned green, and I released the brake, hit the accelerator, and ... stalled. The cars started honking behind me as I tried again—stall number two. After a third stall, I finally got the car moving ... just as the light turned red.

The honking continued, broken up by an occasional "Get out of the way, moron!" I was now losing my nerve but remained determined. And I thought I could drive! The light turned green before I was ready, and I immediately stalled again. Two more stalls and the light was turning red again. I then noticed that the second car behind me was a Baltimore police car, and the officer was now striding beside my vehicle. I almost lost consciousness at this point.

"So, you just got your license, son."

Was it that obvious? He smiled and just said, "Take your time, son. They're just testing their horns out behind you." I'll never forget that officer because I would still be at that light without him, and the street would have been turned into a pedestrian mall. I did stall one more time, and when I finally started moving forward, it was as if I had just stared down certain death. It took me a while to overcome my fear of going into first gear on a hill. Still, ironically, I was one of the last people I know to switch to an automatic transmission, only because the dealer wanted several thousand more for a car with manual transmission. By that time, hills had become my friend. I was invincible! Children today have been spared one of these rites of maturation; everyone should have to learn how to drive a manual transmission.

In the fall of that year. I volunteered to run every errand imaginable, not because I was a good kid, but because I wanted the world to see me driving. I would go out of the way just to pass a friend's house; I was the coolest cat on Earth. Sitting tall in the saddle, I would ride by, pretending not to notice the people I was showing off for. One could drive a younger person around then, and I would take my sister, eighteen months my junior, to her friends' houses. I just soaked it all in, the big brother who could drive! Of course, I would have to drive Gussie's friends around the block. However, this road king was to be quickly dethroned the following January in a day I'll never forget.

I had been driving for four months at this point. The novelty had worn off, but my driving ego had just continued to grow, setting me up for the Big Fall. It had snowed the night before, and I remembered everything Mr. Stevens and my father had told me about driving in slippery conditions. I would continue to be the roadmaster. Dad asked if I could drive him to the hardware store that Saturday, and I was happy to oblige. The roads were virtually snow-free, and parallel parking was no issue; Mr. Stevens had drilled me on that and given me a foolproof system. Dad then suggested we explore the city a little, and we ended up at Memorial Stadium. The Baltimore Colts had played their last game, and the parking lots, completely deserted, were coated with several inches of snow. We started making loops around the massive empty lot, and he told me to accelerate to thirty-five miles per hour. It was a breeze, and he could undoubtedly smell my overconfidence. He suddenly grabbed my arm while screaming, "STOP!" And the car did stop ... after it had done five to six 360o spins. I looked over at Dad, trying to hold back his laughter.

"Maybe we ought to try that again!"

My confidence was showing significant cracks at this point, but after the second series of spins, more spectacular than the first, it was now crumbling. Dad smiled and indicated that everyone had trouble in the snow and ice. We would keep practicing until I could hit the brakes and control the spin. Everyone knew that the one question all got wrong on the written driver's test was which way to turn when a car started to skid to the side. I had that answer down cold turkey when I aced that test four months earlier, but knowledge is no substitute for instinct and experience. I kept telling myself to turn in the same direction that the car's rear was skidding, but every time, my feeble instincts trumped logic. Dad explained that using the brakes sparingly was the key. We practiced, and we spun until I could finally control the spin. Dad was the personification of patience that day, and fifty years later, I still remember that day vividly. The road king was dethroned and finally gave the automobile the respect it deserved.

That day has stuck with me, making me the sound driver I am. I learned that driving was a responsibility and not a privilege. Yes, I could drive, but anytime I forgot how dangerous a vehicle could be, I was to open the door to a potential accident. Thanks. Dad! I still feel you beside me, patiently trusting and guiding. Some things stick with us forever. It's incredible how much we need a parent even when we think we don't.

WITH APOLOGIES TO
GEORGE FRIDERIC HANDEL

Some moments in life are sometimes painful to remember, although time dulls the pain and allows us to see the humor embedded in them. I have had more than my share of embarrassing moments; ripping my pants while on local TV during the dedication of Baltimore's Cathedral of Mary Our Queen has to rank right up there. I was recruited to be an altar server at the church, something I did more out of curiosity than religious inclination. That clothing malfunction went fortunately unnoticed by the masses, although a few close friends thoroughly enjoyed it. Being naturally clumsy, accidents were frequent, and if someone had made a video of Radcliffe's Greatest Mishaps, it would have contended for the comedy special of the year.

My one extracurricular activity was in the school choral group during high school. Although I would never be world-renowned for my singing ability, I did enjoy being a part of a singing group. Pavarotti, I was not. My sixth-grade music teacher had asked me to just mouth the words for a class concert, although my voice was not that bad. My grandmother said I had a lovely voice, but then grandmothers would praise anything you did. She also was seriously hard of hearing at that stage of her life. However, I did enjoy music, and singing in the group was one of my few social activities. I had no exceptional talent, hobby, or interest, and if I hadn't joined at least one school activity, there was a good chance that my classmates would be wondering who I was when I walked across the stage to receive my diploma. The rehearsals got me out of some school activity; that may have been an added incentive.

Ours was a male-only school, a completely unnatural phenomenon since girls become foreign objects rather than real people. Our concerts were done in conjunction with a local girl school to get the needed sopranos and altos. While I was in seventh grade, we joined a local girl school for a day of rehearsals and a concert to be followed by a dance. The girl school contained grades nine through twelve, and some deranged matchmaker paired up boys and girls for the day. I, a prepubescent, shy kid with a crew cut and zero interest in dating, was paired up with a gorgeous seventeen-year-old junior—no computer matchmaking here, but then this predated personal computers by almost twenty years. I felt so sorry for the girl whose day was ruined by that bizarre matching. While she immediately retreated to her friends, to her credit, she did check on me frequently. I'm guessing that day was not the highlight of her school career.

As I aged in years, the concerts with the girl schools became more enjoyable, although shyness prohibited me from engaging any of the girls in significant conversation. One concert was particularly memorable as we sang parts of Handel's *Messiah*. The program ended with the *Hallelujah* chorus, as inspirational a piece of music as there ever was. I had recently attended a full symphony/choral society rendition of this in downtown Baltimore with a friend, and it impressed me. While my music interests tended toward folk, rhythm and blues, and rock, I loved classical music and played it often. Hearing a full orchestra and chorus singing Handel's masterpiece was incredible, and when the whole audience stood for the *Hallelujah*, I honestly was moved. Getting to perform it was going to be the high point of my very brief singing career. We were not going to sing the entire oratorio and practiced the movements we would sing to excess.

Finally, the day of the concert came. I believe I was a tenor, although my memory fails me. However, something else was going to fail me that evening. It had been a long evening, and we were getting to the famous chorus; the musical director was tapping his baton and using his other hand to communicate that this was the work's high point. We all took a breath and got ready for the first note. This is the moment we had all waited for, and even with my mediocre voice, I was prepared to belt out that piece. And that's when IT happened, a nightmare realized. In one of its most dysfunctional moments, my digestive system decided to release a large blast of gas, clearly audible to a sizable portion of the singers and many in the audience, as my anal sphincters vibrated away. The beautiful and inspirational mood in the auditorium was suddenly ripped apart by a series of snickers. Needless to say, the majestic *Hallelujah* began on the most dissonant of notes. I kept thinking, "Why now?" While humorous to many, it also came across as disrespectful. There had been no warning of the impending digestive malfunction, and I still couldn't believe it came from me. This was THE *Hallelujah* chorus; heads of state stood solemnly for this. My ego was battered these days anyway; this would further deflate it, and I suddenly needed to develop a case of severe amnesia.

I think there must be a unique flatulation gene that runs in our family. My mother was clearly above embarrassment as her gaseous explosions would rock the house (at least they seemed that way). My father would always say, "There's a mouse in the house!" or "Who cut the cheese?" We all accepted this as a simple fact of family life. I don't know how many times I would have a friend over when that all too obvious sound would emanate from her second-floor bedroom, from which, I'm sure, she thought no one could hear. If the gases in flatulence are flammable, our lives were in constant danger in that house. A friend in high school tested the flammability theory by using a lighter to ignite a "blast;" I would have loved to have been there while he explained to the nurse why he was unable to sit down in class after the ignited gas reversed direction to fill the created vacuum. What amazed me was that Mom never seemed phased. She would fire these plate-rattling depth charges at the table, oblivious that the rest of us were falling apart in laughter, with my father leading the charge. To my horror, he even bought the family a recording called *The Contest*, a humorous recitation of a flatulation contest with sound effects. I was a little horrified, but my parents loved it. In hindsight, this was one of the ways my parents remained human to me, something which endeared them to me. Needless to say, I never played this record for my friends.

I'll never forget my days as an altar server in the Catholic cathedral in Baltimore. I remember well one service when the priest "let one fly." The other altar server and I were probably the only ones who heard it, but we both cracked up, our amusement coming from not realizing that priests were human also. I tried to stifle my laugh, and just as I would start to get it under control, the other boy would start giggling. We fed off each other the whole service; I'm sure the parishioners thought us disrespectful. I wondered if Christ passed gas also; it certainly might have put a severe damper on the Last Supper or the Sermon on the Mount.

While I can live a happy life without hearing another "fart" joke," a challenging thing to do when one teaches middle school students, there is one aspect of the subject that I enjoy. Sometimes in life, we focus more on our differences than on our commonalities. Still, the core of the humanness we share always shows itself during those intestinal malfunctions, humbling even the most arrogant among us. I still love listening to Handel's *Messiah*, but I must admit that the *Hallelujah* chorus will always be tainted by my memory of that one unfortunately timed note. Years later, no one else remembers the incident, but it seemed a death sentence to that teenager. If only at the dinner that night I had not gone back for that second helping of beans.

THE REAL WIZARDS OF OZ

My Oz had four remarkable wizards, each with a unique brand of magic. Even though I grew up in a home full of love, patience, and genuine caring, I still needed a wizard's magic. A parent's love and time can only extend so far, especially in a home with four children, two with significant medical and psychological issues. I consider myself one of the luckiest persons in the world to have had that loving home and almost daily access to four exceptional wizards, my grandparents. Unlike the Frank Morgan character in *The Wizard of Oz*, there was nothing fake about these four characters who added much joy to my early life. If I were a Christmas tree, my parents would be the ones who built a strong tree, but my grandparents added so many of the ornaments. All four lived within three blocks of my home and were able to step in so many times when jobs and other family responsibilities kept my parents preoccupied. Everyone should be so blessed. With families far more mobile today and the role of grandparents changing, few today have the kind of access I had to my wizards.

Mary McKim Marriott Radcliffe (1881 – 1963), my paternal grandmother, had an advanced degree in spoiling grandchildren, and every child should be spoiled to some extent. She was artistic, eccentric, creative, and loving. Overprotective of my father, she completely reversed directions with her grandson, indulging me with chocolate, gifts, and teddy bears. Days spent at her home were an adventure: exploring her spacious house with more stored in it than a museum. In addition to showering me with treats, unlimited kindness, and marvelous stories, she introduced me to the world of movies. On many afternoons, she would take me by cab downtown to a movie, often returning to see an excellent film a second time; we saw *Around the World in Eighty Days* three times, a long movie for a seven-year-old but also a superb geography primer.

My paternal grandfather, George Lovic Pierce Radcliffe (1877 – 1974), was my history book, a treasure trove of family history and stories. He was a time machine back to earlier days in our family as his stories painted a vivid and detailed portrait of what my ancestors had to endure to enable me to live the extraordinary life I was living. He was also a former United States senator, but he never shared that side with me when I was young. He just wanted to be a grandfather. In 1964, however, he took me to the Fifth Regiment Armory in Baltimore to hear President Lyndon Johnson make a campaign speech. After the address, we went behind the stage to talk to some friends. I was looking around while he was talking when I heard him say, "Let me introduce you to my grandson." As I turned around, there was the President. That was the first time I realized that my grandfather was more than just a grandfather, but that role is what I remember.

He was also Santa Claus in disguise. Not that he gave copious presents, he just wanted to ensure that our Christmas was similar to those he enjoyed as a child. He arrived every Christmas Eve with a farm truck loaded with trees, holly, pine boughs, bayberry, mistletoe, turkeys, pies, and treats. Living in Baltimore, if we couldn't experience the country Christmas he grew up with, then he would just bring the country to the city. He believed in the importance of tradition and ensured that our lives were immersed in it. To many of my friends, gifts made their day special; thanks to my grandfather, we learned that the absolute joy of the holiday lay in the pleasure of reliving tradition with our family.

My maternal grandfather, William Aloysius Boggs (1891 – 1964), was the wizard I knew the least, not from lack of exposure but because he was soft-spoken. He was the poster child for not speaking unless you have something important to say, something I try to model with at least partial success. With a wife and four wonderfully stubborn and social daughters, he couldn't have gotten many words in any way. A veteran of World War I, where he served in France, he was the child of Irish immigrants, his father a "rags to riches" story in Baltimore. He adapted admirably to living in a female-dominated world, the youngest of a large family with five older sisters. But he was so loved and respected. If things got dull, he could interject a comment to get everyone reacting. He often set off my grandmother and her sister with a controversial statement. He would then sit back with his cigar and watch the fireworks with a twinkle in his eye. He was a true gentleman.

He had two hobbies that I readily acquired—a love of books and model trains. His incredible train garden, mostly handmade, and spectacular train set were a high point of every Christmas. In later years I would help him set up this Christmas garden, and as his health declined, he gave me the complete garden and train set to assemble at our home. He, of course, was there to supervise. He also had an incredible library of classics, and I dove into these on my numerous visits: complete sets of Twain, Stevenson, Verne, and Dickens, to name a few. This was recreation for many sizzling summer afternoons or cold, wintry days.

My maternal grandmother, Augusta Heiskell Boggs (1895 – 1978), worked her magic in many ways. She was my guardian angel. I spent many days in that house and sometimes packed a suitcase and walked the three blocks for a weekend visit. Her meals were a trip to heaven after a week of enduring my mother's often failed attempts at cooking. On so many occasions when the world was crashing down on me in my early teens, her home was my safe haven. She never asked questions, offered advice, or passed judgment; she simply served up love and patience. Too often, adults think it is their place to provide advice when what is needed is patience and understanding, to listen non-judgmentally. She performed the same life-saving strategies on my sister, Gussie, who had significant psychological issues by age twelve. However, Gussie was a different person when around our grandmother. It's not that my parents weren't loving; our grandmother just accepted her as she was, no questions asked. Our grandmother Boggs has a seat of honor if there is a heaven. I strive to be as patient as she was but fail regularly.

Remove those four wizards from my Oz, and I am a completely different person. I was blessed to have all four live well into my life and to be in such proximity. I realize few were as fortunate as I was, but then this was a time when a family was defined more broadly than today. Some today do not want to rely on grandparents' help because they either don't want to appear weak or be subjected to unsolicited advice and interference. My parents were wise. They both saw the importance of a larger, richer family, but with two daughters with extreme medical needs, they knew they needed help. We all need that extended family to reinforce the values being taught and expose us to a broader variety of experiences.

I have a treasure trove of memories, and these four unique individuals are woven into many of them. It's sad that when we are older and realize how essential people were in our early lives, they are not around for us to thank. My Oz was crumbling over time, but I had four wizards to carry me through the most challenging days.

The House at Pooh Corner

Wherever they go, and whatever happens to them on the way,
in that enchanted place on the top of the forest,
a little boy and his Bear will always be playing.

— A.A. Milne, *The House at Pooh Corner*

Walking through our house today, you will notice teddy bears everywhere. Cabinets, bookshelves, closets, and chairs are populated with dusty bears of every size and description. My children think I've lost my mind or, more likely, never had one to begin with. Even more absurd is that many of these bears have personalities and "talk," much to Jackie's horror. Am I reverting to my childhood or beginning the long downhill slide to diapers and dementia? The bears are an essential link to a special part of my past. Many leave their childhood behind as a series of memories, but I have incorporated it as a part of me.

Like so many young children, I was given teddy bears when young. My grandmothers gave me bears as presents. Every year, one gave me a Steiff bear, which I wish I still had, and each Christmas, the other gave me a bear that was always larger than the one I got the year before. By age seven, they rivaled me in size. I remember when a friend and I decided to parachute them out the third-floor window of our row house in Baltimore. Chubby Tubby Timmy, the four-foot polar bear, had a defective chute that did not deploy properly. He ended up hanging from a tree about ten feet above our narrow road and had to await rescue by my father when he got home from work. We enjoyed watching cars suddenly slow as they saw a furry monster above the road all day long, rocking gently in the breeze. Several people stopped, puzzled at this beast's sudden appearance. Others traveled up the road a second time to admire the magnificent creature. One terrified older woman even backed out of the long one-way street to avoid an impending attack. It was as marvelous a day as life in the city could provide.

My mother and grandmother regularly read to me from A.A. Milne's Pooh stories, igniting an obsession with bears. They followed me everywhere and, in many ways, were my companions before the family finally got a dog. Years later, in high school, my Latin teacher assigned our class a project of reading and reviewing a book entirely written in Latin. While others flocked to Caesar and Virgil, I retreated to a book given to me by my grandmother, that famous Latin classic, A.A. Milne's *Winnie Ille Pooh*. The teacher never forgave me for this choice, although he had to accept it since it was entirely in Latin.

The bears were my security blanket and provided comfort and considerable amusement. They had names, personalities, and feelings. Childhood imagination knows no bounds, and they all came to life for me. My mother often reminded me that normal people did not talk to stuffed animals. These were not just stuffed animals. However, my bear world took on a whole new dimension with my sister Kim. She was eight years younger than I and mentally disabled. My mother had German measles when she was pregnant with Kim, which was likely the cause.

Kim was difficult for my mother to manage, and after the nurse left at 4:30 PM, I would unofficially take over care of Kim. We would go for walks, play in the side yard, build forts out of scrap lumber, and play ball, but she was most comfortable in my room. The bears became the centerpiece of our little world. We'd build houses out of card tables and sheets and jump in with all the bears. Kim became so special to me, and the bears were how I communicated with her. The time would fly by as we retreated into our little world. She was a challenging child, prone to epic temper tantrums, but in our bear world, this never occurred. I remember vividly having to clean her room one day after she removed her diaper and "finger-painted" the walls, some of the most impressive murals the world has ever seen. Because she could rock to move the crib around the room, her room soon rivaled the Sistine Chapel. I never minded the hours of cleanup, which my mother was delighted to yield to me. I also remember the time that she got under our electric train platform and disconnected hundreds of yards of wiring and the day she unwound a mile of my recorded magnetic tapes. I would get angry, obviously, but soon this would pass, and we would pick up right where we left off. She was the joy of my life.

We'd go for frequent walks, always taking one of the bears in the stroller. There was so much to explore, and we discovered many secret little areas where we could play. Building leaf forts in the fall was always a treat, and of course, a bear had to always join us. I don't know how much of this made an impression on her, but I looked forward to our times together. As it became apparent that Kim was not "normal," I tried harder to help her. I was convinced that if I worked harder, I could make her speak. I spent hours daily working with her, hoping something would stick. Twelve-year-old children feel like they can do anything, and I knew I could get Kim to talk. We bonded, and to this day, those are some of the happiest days I have ever spent. I didn't always know how to deal with her constant temper tantrums, but those never occurred in our bear world. As it turned out, "bear" was the only word she spoke in her life.

Then came a day that was to be a turning point in my life. I raced home from school as I usually did each day. The school was about three-quarters of a mile from our home, and I usually made the trek on foot. The nurse would be leaving soon, and I would take over. My sister, Gussie, would often get home earlier and start without me. I ran in the door that day, and the house was strangely quiet. It was unusual not to encounter one of Kim's temper tantrums. My mother would retreat to her ritual afternoon nap. Taking care of Kim had devastated her, and she was no longer the mother I had known as a young child. The most loving and unselfish mom in the world was now emotionally battered and suffering from bouts of depression. Her bedroom became her retreat as she could no longer manage the emotional or physical strain imposed on her by her youngest child.

That day I knew Mom was in her bedroom as I could hear the television chatter emanating from the room. She was watching the latest crowning of a "Queen for a Day." I went to look for the nurse, whom I figured must be with Kim. Mom had always had a house cleaner come in a couple of times a week to help, but after it became clear that Kim was not going to improve, the cleaner evolved into a nurse who came in from 8 AM to 4 PM. Kim had seemed normal in her first year and a half, but it soon became apparent that she was not progressing intellectually as much as she should and, by age three, was regressing intellectually, putting a severe strain on our household. There were no services available to help families then, and it soon was apparent that Kim was more than my mother could handle. I can only imagine the emotional hurt to my mother, knowing she could no longer manage her child. Kim was a handful, often taking off from the house, outrunning my mother easily. That afternoon I found no sign of the nurse and began to worry. When I went into my mother's bedroom to ask where Kim was, my mother said, "Wait until your father gets home." I walked out puzzled ... and very worried.

Mom would always arise from her "nap" when my father came home between 5:30 and 6:00 PM, and the two would have their evening cocktail. I came down from my room when I heard him enter, asking where Kim was. It was almost unheard of for her to be absent from the home, and I could only suspect the worst. There must have been some accident, but why would my mother not have been with her in the hospital? The two sat me down and explained that Kim had gone somewhere else to live, a home in Glen Burnie for young children with special needs. There had been no hint of this move, and I was utterly stunned. My father explained how this was best for all in the family, but that was little consolation. I began to argue and plead: I could take care of her. As it became apparent that the decision was irrevocable, I dissolved in tears. My precious sister was gone.

I slept little that night, trying to convince myself she was not gone, just living elsewhere. If she could visit, I could adjust. My father indicated that visits could be arranged, and we could see her often. I started to rally, but in succeeding days, returning home from school to that "empty" house forced the stark reality to sink in: Kim was gone. What hurt as much as the loss was that I had been left out of the decision. She was "my Kim," and she had just been taken away. I know my parents were trying to spare me the emotional turmoil, but I'm not sure they realized how essential a part of me Kim was.

It would be months before we would visit Kim, and when we returned a second time to see her at Christmas, she seemed to have forgotten me. That was as devastating a moment as I have ever experienced. Kim was standing right before me, but she was gone … never to return. I gazed into those remarkable blue eyes, but there was no hint of any recognition. Angel's Haven, the home which took her in, was marvelous, but I knew where her real home should be. Kim never visited after that, and I realized I had lost her. My whole life imploded that year, and I was not equipped emotionally to deal with it. We never talked about Kim at home, and I could not understand why a vital part of our family had just been forgotten. Nothing could fill the void I felt, and I soon lost my interest in the bears. They now no longer could come to life in front of me. Later that year, I returned home another day to find the bears now gone, disposed of by my parents, who now thought me too old to have them and wanted to reduce clutter, … and clutter reigned supreme in my room. The damage was complete, and I suddenly fell into a deep "sleep" from which I would awaken many years later.

From age twelve on, everything declined. I had fewer friends, my work habits and grades dropped markedly, and loneliness set in. The mild stuttering, which had been a part of me for several years, became completely debilitating, and I closed off in school. Over the next few years, I sank from being one of the top two or three in my class to residing near the bottom. I struggled to cope with an ever-changing social world. With the bears and Kim both gone, a large piece of me was missing. It would be a while before the void would be filled again. Early adolescence is not an easy time in any person's life, and I had the usual doubts and awkwardness. But looking back on these days, a part of me was missing; I started becoming someone that was not me.

After years of struggling to cope and fill the loneliness, I began to recover what I had lost. I found at the summer camp, where I was a counselor, that working with children was hitting the right chord,

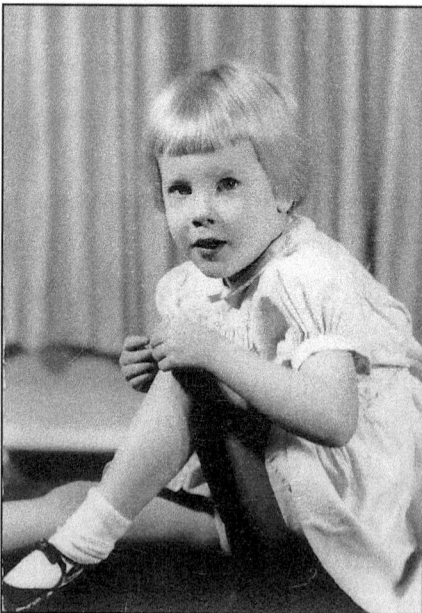

Mary McKim Radcliffe
1957-1975

and in 1969 when I met Jackie, the healing began. With her and later with my children, the bears returned. We still have Eddie Tubbs, the bear I gave Jackie in the hospital in 1972 after her miscarriage. Beagle Bailey recently chewed off the nose, and the poor bear has lost 95% of the fuzz he ever had, but Jackie knows we can't throw it away. I'll be the first to tell you how ridiculously silly that is. It's just a piece of cheap material filled with even cheaper stuffing. But you can't throw away memories; I did that once before.

I periodically would have low points well into adulthood, never wholly understanding how all the pieces fit together. I had filed memories of Kim deep into the recesses of my mind and wasn't seeing the connection between her and the bears. Maybe it was just a question of trying to recapture a lost childhood, but I was happiest when that lost little boy could come alive. A part of being a whole person is to keep all the facets of who we are and have been. Not that we want to stay a child, but one does not have to reject childhood to become an adult. Some people throw away who they are to become the adult they think they should be. They become an incomplete person. It's easy to see that something is missing in them, and often they discover too late what they have lost.

We all search for who we are, and many spend a lifetime searching but never finding. In growing and maturing, we are evolving, not replacing one self with another. The child is full of fear and insecurity but loaded with hopes, dreams, and imagination. As adults, we are better able to make rational decisions, but we are still the child at the core. To reject that core is to drift aimlessly through life. To keep one's inner child is to remain open-minded, to be able to look outside the box, to retain a degree of spontaneity, and to remember what is profoundly important.

Kim passed away over forty-five years ago from pneumonia, neglected in her final days in an institution. Jackie and I visited her right before she died, and there was still no recognition of me. I no longer knew the person who was standing in front of me. It was hard to know what to feel—sadness over what could have been, guilt at not spending more time with her after she left, but also joy over what were four of the happiest years of my life. I might have lost her, but the little boy was starting to mend, a process that would still take many years. I have only a few pictures of her which I treasure.

I can only imagine how difficult this all was for my parents. This happened when no services were available to help mentally impaired children, and institutionalization was the only option. Mom and Dad did what they thought was best for the family, and "giving up" a child had to be almost crippling.

Kim is still with me, however. It took many years to bring her back to life. She sits there as one of the many bears that now adorn our home. They will always be a part of me and a memorial to her. Pooh lives on with our grandchildren in written word and stories, and I inflict the "bear world" on them with the exploits of the inhabitants of this little world. Jackie is remarkably understanding. It's a tricky thing to explain to someone. As an adult, I recognize the reality of a cheap assemblage of cotton and mohair, but it's what they represent. I can't let them die again. Or should I say, I refuse to die again? I may have left Oz far behind, but the child in me reigns strong. I still and will always reside at the House at Pooh Corner.

❖ ❖ ❖

But, of course, it isn't really Good-bye, because the Forest will always be there... and anybody who is Friendly with Bears can find it.

— A.A. Milne, *The House at Pooh Corner*

DIXIE, I'VE A FEELING WE'RE NOT IN OZ ANYMORE!*

*I*was again heading with Dixie to a spot I had frequented many times. Kim had accompanied me years earlier, but Dixie was now my faithful companion. We climbed up a small trail in our neighborhood and descended to the foundation of an old garage, now entirely covered by shrubs and vines. Here I was safe; no one could see or hear me. It was my escape, where Dixie and I could talk. Yes, beagles do talk if one knows how to listen.

"Come here, Dixie; I've got a dog biscuit for you." Dixie would do anything for a treat. "You're the best dog ever." Dogs also have egos that need to be massaged. She was smiling and watching me closely. While likely waiting for another biscuit, I imagined she eagerly awaited what I would say.

"Today was the worst day ever, although I think that's what I said yesterday. I thought I did well on that history essay, but I got a C. Mr. Smith obviously doesn't like me. I don't think I could ever do something that he would like. I used to love school. I don't fit in; now; I don't think there's even one teacher who knows that I exist. I met with the college counselor today, and he said that I'll never get into my choices unless I get my grades up."

Dixie wagged her tail as if she understood everything I said.

"When I try to study, my mind wanders. This past week has been worse, with Gussie missing. She's been gone for five days, and Mom and Dad are

---

* This allusion to *The Wizard of Oz* (1939) is based on Dorothy's often misquoted line to her dog, Toto.

frantic. She's run away before, but this is the longest she has been gone. She called the second day from some hotel downtown but was gone when Dad went to get her. Bill seems oblivious to it all, or at least he seems that way. He always seems carefree."

"I was looking through the family photo album last night. It's fun looking back on those early years. Everything seemed so simple back then, and even Gussie seemed happy. Why has everything gotten so complicated? Everyone seemed so carefree then; Mom was always smiling. I liked looking at the few pictures we have of Kim, but I haven't seen her in over a year now. She would be eight now, and would I even recognize her? None of my friends back then are still friends. It's like the world has gone on and left me behind."

Dixie, sensing my mood, was beside me now with her head on my leg. I stroked her belly, and her eyes were currently closed. I knew she wasn't sleeping because she'd squeeze in closer when my tears started to flow. How nice it would be to be a beagle—to have all these problems fade away. Waving another dog biscuit under her nose, she took it without even opening her eyes.

"The dance is coming up, and I'll have to ask someone to go. Who would want to go with me? And then I'd have to talk to her, and what would we say? I always enjoyed Gussie's friends when they came over, but everything is different now. Most of her friends don't come over now that she's having trouble. I can't be the only one who doesn't go to the dance, but it will be so uncomfortable."

Dixie was such a comfort—non-judgmental and attentive to my every mood. She liked me the way I was. And yes, dogs can talk. The most meaningful communication was nonverbal—words were often a smoke screen for what one truly felt—and Dixie always knew the right thing to say. She was now licking me. One could pretend that this was a beagle kiss, even if she was just searching for a stray crumb. I would have to go home at some point as Mom would be organizing dinner. Maybe Dad would barbecue tonight, giving us a break from TV dinners. But I felt safe here.

At age 16, I was terrified of the future yet strengthened by the past. I was always trying to feel sorry for myself. Indeed, there seemed to be no more pathetic creature alive. I was a poor athlete, now a weak student, and hardly noticed in a small class. I felt inadequate and unprepared for the future, but wonderful memories would quickly derail my journey into self-pity.

Oz gave its inhabitants a zest for life and the initiative and tools to transform any day. A day would begin with no plan and soon turn magical as we imagined, created, and built. There was no Disneyworld, vacations were simple, if they would happen at all, and television was limited, if we even had it. We needed little. I knew those days were behind me, but they were my core. My tree was strong even if most of the ornaments had fallen off. I wanted to wallow in self-pity, but honesty made me realize how blessed I was. Few could boast of the album of childhood memories I possessed.

Yes, I grew up in Oz, but both personal setbacks and events in the world around me brought down the curtain on that magical place. The world seemed to unravel as the threat of nuclear war with the Soviet Union became a staple of the evening news. And in 1963, President Kennedy, the wizard of the country's version of Oz, was assassinated. That was shortly after Kim had left our home, and Gussie began exhibiting significant problems.

I petted Dixie, who seemed utterly relaxed. Oh, to be a dog whose only worry is waiting for the next meal.

"I get mad when I start feeling sorry for myself. I think my problems are worse than anyone's, but then I look at some others, and I feel silly. We're not poor; I have a family and am healthy. I have so much to be thankful for; then why do I feel so miserable? I wish it were summer because I could escape to the camp again. I like working with the kids and don't feel stupid there. I can relax there, and I feel appreciated. And I get away from the stress of the home."

I didn't realize this was a premonition of a future career. I had told everyone my entire life that I wanted to be a doctor. When asked what I wanted to be when I grew up, I had to say something, and this sounded impressive. In reality, I had no clue what I wanted to do. It didn't occur to me at the time that my enjoyment and success as a camp counselor would lead me to a successful career in teaching.

"Dixie, I've got to ask someone to the dance. But will anyone want to go with me? Most of my friends are dating and going to parties, while I sit at home feeling like a misfit. And I stutter. I'll have to call since there is no one I am likely to run into. Maybe tomorrow. But I said that yesterday."

Dixie was sitting up now. She was like a pay phone; add another dog biscuit to be able to listen for another ten minutes.

I was struggling with the fear of moving ahead when my life in Oz had been so uncomplicated. I felt guilty that I had lived such a pampered existence, but I knew I had to move on. I didn't realize that I was far stronger than I thought. While Oz might not have prepared me to live in the 1960s, it gave me all the tools I needed to adapt. The strength I couldn't see was built on the love of a family. Our family of six was dysfunctional in some ways, but all we knew was love and support.

We can never know what lies around the corner. I was four years away from meeting the person who would forever change my life. Jackie, my future wife, would give my life the stability it lost as problems temporarily unraveled my childhood family.

Even then, there was a peace inside me from those early days in Oz—the same feeling one gets when curling up under the covers on a frosty winter evening. One does need to eventually shed the covers, get up, and face the world, but the comfort has a therapeutic value; it reenergizes us. While living in the real world now, I keep Oz nearby—the teddy bears adorning our home, the beagle sitting in my lap, and the extensive multi-sensory photo album engrained in me. Dixie, we're not in Oz anymore, but I carry it everywhere.

I had been quiet for a while now, and Dixie was beginning to stir.

Standing up, she gave me the patented beagle stare. I knew exactly what this meant.

"Dixie, you want dinner, don't you?" Her tail wagged even faster now. "I guess it is time to get home now. Mom will be firing up the oven to cook those TV dinners. If she overcooks it again, you'll get a second dinner."

Dixie led the way out of the garage as we emerged into the sunlight. It was back to the real world now, and though nothing out there had changed, I was ready to face life again. I would call someone tonight for the dance, and I guess I could survive another day in school.

"Dixie, you're the best doggie ever."

But she was in dinner mode and heading back down the trail. Nothing had changed, but peace was restored.

EPILOGUE:

THE PICTURE ON THE STAIRCASE REVISITED

The other day, I encountered someone I had known as a child but had not seen for many years. They asked about my family, and I told them they had all died. With a horrified expression, they immediately apologized for asking, feeling they had brought up a taboo subject. They next made a comment that struck a chord, "So now you're an only child." Their reaction and statement evoked two strong responses. First, I certainly didn't mind talking about deceased family members. I then strongly reacted, "I am NOT an only child." They were taken aback by my strong reaction, and I had to explain. "I still have a brother and two sisters. They are a part of me, and I think of them daily. They live on in the memories and stories, and to forget them would make me an only child."

They responded, "I'm sorry you had to go through all of this."

"Don't be sorry. The grief tells me that they live on in me. I take comfort in it, knowing they are not forgotten. I am so much richer to have had them in my life. If I had been an only child, I would have been spared the grief, but to be deprived of all the joy they brought me would be a real tragedy."

Many believe happiness is the absence of grief; instead, it puts everything in the proper perspective. I look at that photo on the staircase daily and realize how blessed I have been. Oz remains a real place for me, and as its ambassador, I will walk forward empowered by solid memories and the love of a remarkable family.

www.ingramcontent.com/pod-product-compliance
Lightning Source LLC
Chambersburg PA
CBHW070945150426
42812CB00067B/3318/J